THE GUARDIANS

An Elegy

SARAH MANGUSO

GRANTA

Granta Publications, 12 Addison Avenue, London W11 4QR

First published in Great Britain by Granta Books 2012
First published in the US in 2012 by Farrar, Straus and Giroux

A CIP catalogue record for this book is available from the British Library.

1 3 5 7 9 10 8 6 4 2

ISBN 978 1 84708 310 4

Designed by Jonathan D. Lippincott

Offset by M Rules

Printed and bound by CPI Group (UK) Ltd, Croydon, CR0 4YY

All signs are misleading.
—Yiddish proverb

THE GUARDIANS

The Thursday edition of the *Riverdale Press* carried a story that began *An unidentified white man was struck and instantly killed by a Metro-North train last night as it pulled into the Riverdale station on West 254th Street.*

The train's engineer told the police that the man was alone and that he jumped. The police officers pulled the body from the track and found no identification. The train's 425 passengers were transferred to another train and delayed about twenty minutes.

·

If I were a journalist I'd have spoken to everyone and written everything down right away. I'd have gone to the hospital and met all the people who were on the psychiatric ward at the moment Harris walked out the door, and then this book would be a more accurate rendering of the truth.

If I were to write responsibly, with adequate research to confirm certain facts, I'd have to ask people about the last time they saw or spoke with or heard from my friend Harris. I'm afraid to ask his parents those questions. I'm afraid to talk with his last lover. I'm afraid to meet his doctors and the man who drove the train.

For three years I've studied klezmer orchestration, the physics of rainstorms, maps of Eastern Europe. I thought I could trade my life for this useless, vigorous research. Since I was afraid to know so many answers, I didn't ask any questions, and now it's been three years. Now no one could possibly be able to remember the mundanities of July 23, 2008.

I could have waited until the end of my life to try to understand what happened on that day, saved it for last so I could know its whole effect, but instead I waited what seems an arbitrary, meaningless length of time.

I tried so hard not to notice Harris's death, I barely remember it. Time eroded the memory of it even as it gathered the dust of what's happened since. But I need to try to remember it now so I might keep it from haunting me.

•

We know the lost time begins just after noon because that's what the desk nurse said, and we know it ends at 10:48 because that's when the train pulled into the station. Sometime during that minute, maybe the engineer engaged the air brake. Maybe he blew the whistle. And before or after the engineer did those things, the train's snub nose, or maybe its whole underside, just above the rails, made contact with my friend's still living body.

I want to say that ten hours are missing from Harris's life, but that isn't right. They were in his life. They just weren't in anyone else's.

Though I wish I could, I can't say Harris lay down on the train track and felt relief. I can't imagine anything but torment, a blinding light, then nothing.

What I carry now—it brightens sometimes, without warning—is not his pain. This pain is mine, and unlike my friend, I don't try to hide it. I let it get all over everything. I yell in my studio. I cry on the subway. I tell everyone I know that my friend threw himself under a train.

•

Some people believe that only the selfish accept suicide as a possibility, but I don't believe suicide is available to everyone. It was available to me for a moment, and then a door shut between me and it. The door has stayed shut.

Some people think I should be angry at Harris, but I'm not angry. I believe in the possibility of unendurable suffering.

A man whose lover died slowly wants this book to be about love.

A man whose brother died quickly wants this book to be about rage. *I couldn't save my brother*, he says. *It never goes away*, he says.

●

Sometimes I wish someone else had died instead—someone who blocks the open subway doors, for example, or someone who leaves piles of peanut shells on a train car. The fantasy comes to me in a flash—*I can bring him back to life!*

The woman who changed her baby's diaper and left the filth on an orange plastic subway seat—I'd have traded her for Harris. And I'd have traded the man who unwrapped a candy, placed it in his mouth, dropped the wrapper on the platform in front of his feet, chewed, unwrapped another candy, placed it in his mouth, dropped the wrapper on the platform in front of his feet, chewed.

●

Harris played music, wrote software, wrote music, learned to drive, went to college, went to bed with girls, moved to New York, moved to California, went to graduate school, moved back to New York, went to more graduate school. His three psychotic breaks occupied almost no part of his actual life.

During the first episode, he hired a lawyer, convinced his colleagues were conspiring against him. He called his sister, not knowing where he was, thinking he might have been slipped something. She told him to lie down and rest. He called himself an ambulance, sent it away, drove himself to a gas station, parked the car, got out, slept behind a trash bin. A talking dog appeared and told him to enter a house. The door was unlocked. The people inside called the police, and Harris was arrested and brought to the hospital. After thirty-six hours of telephone calls his mother found him.

I don't know what breed of dog it was. I don't know what color the house was. I don't know how the doorknob felt in my friend's hand.

After the first episode, sometimes he'd stop speaking before the end of a sentence.

•

During the second episode, a year after the first, he disappeared from a roof party, and for a horrible moment it was believed he had jumped. Someone went to his house and knocked on the door for a long time before Harris finally opened it, his fist clenched and ready to strike. Days passed. He broke a date to see a play. A cousin came to Brooklyn late at night to fetch him. Knowing he was on the way to the hospital in the morning, Harris ran away from his cousin's house, and the police committed him.

During the third episode, a year after the second, he left his girlfriend. He took a cab to the hospital with an aunt. He went willingly. He knew what was happening.

He was nauseated. He might have been dehydrated. He wasn't sedated.

Then there are ten hours unaccounted for.

He liked whitefish. He liked drinking Manhattans.

He timed his jump in front of the train, and that's the story.

•

During college, five of us squatted at someone's father's house in Cambridge all summer. The father would have disapproved, so when the cleaners came each week to dust and to water the plants, we packed our things and moved them into the closets and stayed out of the house until nighttime. I lived in the daughter's room and replaced her stuffed animals on the bed each week according to a diagram I'd drawn.

I worked at a publishing house, writing summaries of accounting textbooks. The office was freezing, so I took a brown sweater from my friend's father's closet and hung it in my cubicle and put it on every day. I don't remember cleaning it.

Sometimes I went out for drinks with the other interns, who anticipated becoming full time employees of the firm after graduation. They bought office clothes—blazers, shells, hose—with their earnings or with some other money.

Of my four housemates, Harris was the only one with a job. The others watched television, drank watermelon coladas, and sunbathed on the roof. One of them often said in a heavy German accent, *We are not watching the television; we are reading it.*

I don't remember shaking Harris's hand for the first time, and we didn't learn how to talk to each other for a few more years, but I remember our workers' kinship.

•

When college was over, we all moved to New York. Harris's mother cosigned a lease for a loft apartment in Manhattan, on Chambers Street, and for the next decade, a lot of people we knew lived there for a week or a month or a few years.

The third-floor loft, a photographer's former studio, was fourteen hundred square feet and had a small bathroom with a door, a tiled area with a refrigerator and a stove, and a smaller area in the opposite corner, about four by six feet, raised eight inches with some plywood.

I bought some cheap red velvet and hand-sewed a curtain to surround those twenty-four square feet and mounted a bar on the two open edges. I hung my clothing on wire hangers begged from the dry cleaner around the corner, borrowed a narrow futon and a plastic crate from Harris, and lived there for two and a half months.

My ten-foot-high window looked south onto the World Trade Center. It was so close I didn't need to think about it. When I woke up, it was there, filling the window with its mirrors.

My roommates paid more rent than I did and lived in office cubicles separated by drywall. It was more than a year before anyone figured out how to put up a ceiling. As we fell asleep at night, we spoke to each other in the dark like brothers and sisters. Sometimes someone played music in his cubicle so we all could hear it.

After a while we instituted a rule against that, trying to force the illusion of privacy.

Eventually everyone just called the place Chambers Street. We all knew it was No. 119. Keys were given away and lost. Things fell into the floorboard holes. Drugs got stolen. Tenants came and went and their artifacts accumulated—a framed drawing, a piggy bank, a bong. Someone brought home a puppy. Someone put on a nitrous oxide puppet show. Someone dropped the air-conditioning unit out the back window and through a grocery storefront. Someone published a novel about the place. Someone tried to hang himself in the bathroom.

Every New Year's Eve was like the last moment of your life—if you stayed late enough, within a few hours you'd see everyone you'd ever met, minus a few relatives.

Wire-reinforced windows opened onto the fire escape at the front of the building. I sang in a choir and practiced my parts out there, in the cacophony of traffic. I never felt anyone watching me or listening to me as I sang Mendelssohn into the air, three floors up.

After he built his ceiling and bought the orchestral score of a Webern opera, Harris invited me into his room. It wasn't a cubicle anymore. I muddled my way through the soprano line of some song, and he looked at me as if it had been the best thing he'd ever heard.

•

Harris met the train with his body, offered it his body.

The train drove into his body. It drove against his body.

It sent him from his body.

The conductor went down onto the track and touched the body and lifted and carried the body.

There was no need for a doctor.

The body was removed from the track and rested for two days without its name.

•

Engineers who have driven suicide trains, who have looked into the eyes of the people they were forced to kill, aren't required to disembark to remove the remains from the track. Removing the remains is the conductor's job.

My lab partner from ninth-grade biology, now an emergency doctor, writes:

I'm not sure that anyone can tell exactly what happens to a body upon impact with a train. It happens very fast, and it's hard for me to imagine that the person has any awareness of pain because the trauma will likely be so massive and so instant with the amount of force a fast-moving train carries. I don't think any more specific data exists than that it is essentially a massive and rapid crush injury to all organs, bones, etc.

In photographs of bodies hit by cars and crushed by bus tires, train wheels, and tanks, I can see that all the red and yellow interior parts of the body have been pressed out of the skin. The hard skull is detached. The clothes are shredded. The soft inner parts of the body cover a surprisingly large area on the ground.

If I worked in a morgue, I wouldn't expose the entire extruded mess. I'd show the identifier a small part of it, whatever still resembled the outside of a body, or what the identifier might remember of the outside of it, if I could.

I think I remember hearing that Harris's parents identified the body, but then I think the teeth must have been collected, and maybe no one had to look at what was left of Harris's body after it was crushed into its constituent parts.

Thus untethered, the body no longer possessed situation in the world, and there was nothing more to say about it.

•

Harris never listened to music on the subway, he told me, because he liked to hear the sounds of the city: the high sound of metal on metal, the low sound of cars moving forward, the tinny leakage of other people's music from tiny speakers, speech in improbable languages, the breath and movement of bodies, and the live music sung and played by the anonymous performers of the New York City underground.

When the first few bars of a piece of music stayed in my head for months, in my misery I sang them to Harris—and he immediately said, *Oh, that's the fugue to the Bach G minor violin sonata.*

•

Hours into a blind date I looked at my watch, knowing I'd never see the man again but feeling wrecked by the number of first dates I'd had in the past month, and thought, *Why not bring him to the concert?* The redheaded man photographed well but in person had the yellow skin of a vagrant because he'd smoked for thirty years. Thirty years! I'd been accepting dates with older men because I wanted to be taken seriously.

It felt so good to know that Harris's family was there at the concert, waiting for me in case I needed them.

The redheaded man and I went to a concert where Harris was playing fiddle with one of his innumerable bands, and I sat with Harris's mother and introduced the man I'd never see again and basked in the warm light of the underground club.

•

Those blind dates brought me such pleasure—not the pleasure of meeting people, but the pleasure of my pretense that I was trying.

I went out with an actor who sat in a famous person's restaurant and snarled that he hated the famous person, hoping to summon him to the table so they might be photographed together.

I went out with a theater set-builder who had a black belt in something. He grabbed my wrists just before the check came.

I went out with a disc jockey who dragged a leg. Someone had recently approached him in a parking lot at dusk, asked him, *Is that neurological?* and then mugged him.

•

As we pulled into the driveway on the first night of Passover, having taken a car all the way from the city to his parents' house on Long Island, Harris said, *Be careful—my grandmother will think I got married.* We smiled.

We spent all our money on drinks and taxicabs. We knew that others our age had enslaved themselves to mortgages and pregnant wives. Family was a balm for the unimaginative, a consolation for the unremarkable, just another thing to feel superior to.

As if Harris didn't know any better than to eat a cracker before offering one to his girl, his grandmother pointed to the olive spread and said to him, *Make a nice one for Sarah.* What we didn't know, of course, was that the grandmother understood. She just pretended not to. She had seen it all before.

When I was older I understood that I'd been invited into the family and that I'd been too frightened to accept the invitation.

·

On a summer afternoon Harris suggested that he and I go outside for a moment, away from the music and the crowd.

He brought me outside. The sun burned. We stood by the side of a building and I talked about something until Harris knew he wouldn't be able to talk about what he'd brought me outside to talk about. We went back inside.

·

I really wish I could show you my penis, he said, as if it were a painting or a country. *God, I just wish I could show it to you.*

It was said to be a majestic organ, the greatest that many had seen.

We still lived with three other guys in that raw loft space, and at home I turned my gender most of the way off so that when the guys evaluated women, I could listen and even participate a little, and not just fall to pieces at the irrelevance of my femininity. I listened to the dick jokes and cruel anecdotes and judgments and didn't feel a thing. Not for years.

A few women had confirmed among themselves the supremacy of Harris's penis. Eventually we all accepted it into our reality along with another roommate's hairline, another's whining. Harris was the one with the ear for music, the folding bike, and the penis.

Aside from a couple of intoxicated kisses, Harris and I never attempted to touch each other, so his penis was always safe from the responsibility of its power. We could talk about it as if it were an amazing restaurant in another town.

For years, we returned, yearningly, to the subject of the transcendent penis. Each time we discussed it, we observed our feelings—would it be possible that I could be shown the beautiful thing? Could either of us recover from it? And if we couldn't recover, would it be worth it, just to have beheld it for a moment?

If we'd ever been to bed, we could never have talked about his penis as we did.

Now it is among the great mysteries.

•

I lived in Manhattan for six months and then moved to Brooklyn, near the East River, and awoke after the planes had already hit the buildings. There was no tele-vision. The transmitter was in Manhattan in a pile on the ground.

As I got dressed and packed my camera, Harris rang up.

A giant white bank of plume spread east, from Lower Manhattan, across the otherwise blue sky.

We walked to the river. On the other side of it, one building stood where there had been two, and I took two pictures of the fire at the top of it.

People waited quietly along Kent Avenue. Car radios played every couple of blocks, and Harris and I stood in the street, waiting and listening and watching the tower burn.

We didn't stare at the tower as if it were television. We looked at it, looked away, talked a little. People were jumping out of it like angels.

A woman near me screamed, *Oh my God, oh God, oh my God, oh my God*, and whole lives passed before I under-stood that the tower was falling. I watched its hundreds of glass windows shimmer to the ground.

The roof fell neatly downward, erasing floor after floor, like an accordion, but I remember this only because I remember thinking *shimmer* and *accordion*.

Of course there are several films of the buildings fall-ing down, and I could go online right now and watch them, but as far as I know none was taken from Kent Avenue, where we were standing.

Harris walked me home, his left arm around me. All the subway trains in Manhattan had stopped. Some of the stations were filled with corpses, with fire.

We walked to Greenpoint and rode the G train to Long Island City, and rode the Long Island Railroad to Jamaica and then to New Hyde Park, where Harris's mother fetched us and drove us to Great Neck.

She cooked steaks and opened a bottle of American wine, and we ate candy and watched Manhattan on television.

The next day Harris and I went to the beach with a couple of friends staying nearby with another set of parents. The waves were enormous. I lost my sunglasses and was thrown ashore. A red bruise swelled on my hip.

The act of war occupied the reported news all day, just that one story, so we swam through the gale. On a different day we'd have noticed the water was too choppy to swim.

And of course the whole memory of that morning has been written over with what has happened since: My friend, who stood with me and helped me, who hugged me as we walked back toward the city from the river shore, is dead.

•

Two days after the attack, I went home to Brooklyn.

I dropped off my bags and went to the video store around the corner from my apartment. So many people had rented movies, there were no more boxes to hold the cassette tapes. I carried a cassette home in a plastic bag.

It rained hard that night. The bodies started decomposing faster. Fighter planes cut through the sky at all hours.

•

Built in 1912, the New York City General Post Office building's long cornice reads *Neither snow nor rain nor heat nor gloom of night stays these couriers from the swift completion of their appointed rounds.*

I seldom had time to wait in the long lines at the main post office, so when I needed to mail something in that neighborhood, I usually rode the escalator to the top floor of Macy's, where there is a postal depot, as I did on September 14, 2001.

Partway up, the door opened and a weeping woman entered. She wasn't wearing shoes. I pressed the button for the top floor and she screamed at me to send the elevator to the lobby.

Macy's was being evacuated. The area had been patrolled closely for the past two days by police, bomb-sniffing dogs, and fighter jets flying above the avenues.

We went outside, the woman screaming behind me, and all Thirty-fourth Street was filled with people. In the midst of it, people sold American flags on the sidewalks of almost every block.

I ran downtown, away from Times Square, calling my mother in Massachusetts from pay phones every few blocks, asking her to turn on the television and tell me where the bomb was, because no one seemed to know, but it was a false alarm.

•

One month after the attack, while I rode the subway to the office of the *New York Post* for my first day of work on the night shift, the United States and Britain launched air strikes in Afghanistan.

I didn't work on the cover story, whose headline was *Tali-BAM!*

I was assigned the article about the Franciscan rite of the blessing of animals, which also happened that day. All the depressed rescue dogs were brought to the church and taken up to the altar.

At St. Bartholomew's, a bald eagle led the procession, followed by the police and rescue dogs. The article accompanied a picture of a bloodhound named Chase sitting at the altar to receive his blessing, so I wrote the caption *Heavenly Hound*.

Six weeks after the attack, at the site no one spoke. The crater was still smoldering, and its poison smell filled the air. Some people wore gas masks and some didn't. They walked among each other like the uniformed members of opposing teams.

Some of the stores in the neighborhood were open and clean. Others had been abandoned. Makeshift bars crossed a lingerie shop's broken windows, the panties in the vitrines scattered and covered with an inch of fluffy gray dust. My black coat and shoes were gray, too. The fire trucks drove the streets unwashed and covered with red names drawn in the dust with a finger.

After the press conference when he was asked *How many?* and he answered *More than any of us can bear*, the mayor assumed the charisma of a movie star.

The fire burned until February, and by then the Stars and Stripes had sprung up all over the city, a tricolor weed nourished on ambient fear.

•

A few months later, *Bacillus anthracis*, the bacterium that causes anthrax, was found in postal sorting facilities in New Jersey.

A tiny literary magazine in Iowa, where I used to work, stopped opening its mail, but at the *New York Post*, business continued unchanged. I worked at the news desk on the sixth floor. The Op-Ed department, on the other side of the floor, had recently been posted one of several bacteria-laden letters.

The powdered bacteria, still on the floor where it had fallen out of its envelope, was covered by a plastic sheet that an EPA representative had put there. The EPA had judged the granules neither light nor fine enough to float in the air and be inhaled, so everyone returned to work and just avoided walking near the plastic sheet.

Only one person in the whole company had anthrax, and she was the assistant who had opened the letter. On her finger, a lesion wept. I asked the copy chief whether he or the other copy editors were on Cipro, the antibiotic I'd heard about on all the news programs.

No, just Op-Ed, he said.

•

The city was wrapped in a paper shroud. Handmade flyers depicting the thousands of the missing covered its lampposts, phone booths, and walls. Within a few days they were streaked and soggy, and within a few weeks many were pulp, but people kept hanging fresh layers.

Right after the planes hit the buildings, it was assumed

that thousands of victims were staggering uptown from the site or lying unidentified in hospitals, but the last survivor was found on September 12.

The living choked on pulverized cement, asbestos, and ash.

A school in Connecticut was rumored to have lost forty fathers.

It was easy to find someone to go to bed with, do drugs with, or leave town with.

On September 19, the subway map was reprinted with an empty space downtown from Franklin Street to Wall Street. Nine stations were closed. More than a year passed before any of them reopened.

In all the bars were stacks of blue cards reading *New York Needs Us Strong*, with a toll-free number on the back. *If you need to talk, help is available.*

I found my roommate's sister sobbing in my studio one day and thought—maybe this is it, the moment that New York needs us strong! I called the toll-free number on the back of the card and handed her the phone. The person on the other end asked her if she'd had to miss work because of stress, trauma, depression, grief—I don't know which words she used.

My roommate's sister was a poet. She modeled for art students when she needed cash. The person on the phone didn't have anything to say to anyone whose grief wasn't further damaging the economy of a grieving city. The conversation ended.

Even during the summer of the blackout, two years later, the city was hungover from the attack. I walked from Chelsea to Bed-Stuy, four hours in wet heat. In the East Village I saw a woman lying facedown on the sidewalk, screaming. People stood by her, looking exhausted, looking away.

At night I could hear gunshots on Atlantic Avenue and could see the two beams of blue light at Ground Zero from my little studio in the back of the apartment.

•

I was in my apartment, absolutely alone, when I heard of a famous writer's fatal jump from the Staten Island Ferry, and I got up and stood in a doorway, holding myself up by the door frame. I remember wondering when I'd arisen and walked to the threshold. With the writer's drowning I'd advanced one lurid death closer to my own.

I wrote my obituary soon after my college graduation. It seemed as necessary as knowing my Social Security number. I edited it from time to time, adding the names of books and towns. I also wrote the note that would be found with my corpse. For years I saved it in my file so it would be there when I needed it, but I don't need it anymore. Now I save it to remember how far I have traveled from that place where no help comes.

Last year a colleague of mine, someone I'd been out to drink with more than once, someone I'd talked to about his poems and my own, put the barrel of a shotgun in his mouth and pulled the trigger. Afterward I felt an echo of that old feeling—that the line was moving, that I was now one death closer to the threshold—but it was a faint echo. I've felt insulated from my death since I began taking this new medicine. I am no longer moved to write poetry, but I traded poetry for a longer life. I knew I was doing it.

I used to believe that death would come when I was ready to walk through the last door. When I was done with suffering, I'd just open the door and walk through it. I still believe it, but now I believe that someone or something else will open the door.

•

Harris and I sat in McCarren Park on a sunny afternoon. Maybe we'd bought ice cream. It was very hot, so hot that I was wearing only a dress and rubber sandals. I carried my house key and nothing else, just walked up Bedford to meet my friend on the dusty lawn.

We lay on the grass until it was almost dark and Harris

mentioned a dance party in Queens. I couldn't go because I didn't have a sweater for the air-conditioned train or proper shoes or my wallet or anything. It was so hot, I wasn't even wearing underwear.

Harris convinced me to go with him to the party, that he'd take care of my subway fare and anything I needed. Our friend Victor had just died. I felt sad, but most of all I felt safe. Now that Victor was dead I could ride the G train at night without underwear. Now that Victor was dead, I would never die. We were done dying, we who had spoken or written to Victor the week he died. We were twenty-eight, twenty-nine, thirty. Victor had exhausted our tragedy quota. It would be a long time before anyone else would have to die.

·

When Harris was accepted to graduate school and had to move from New York to California, he phoned me, desperate.

In his file drawers I found a mash of bills, old mail, receipts, paper napkins, concert tickets, books, letters, shoes, and packets of crackers. We sorted it and packed it. I cleaned the sink and the toilet and the tub. He let me sort his tax documents, love letters, and everything one finds in a drawer if one takes no care to keep anything in particular out of that drawer.

He had a lot of drawers in that apartment since he'd replaced his wooden furniture with lateral file cabinets. The drawers were big and deep, and they contained everything he owned. I'm glad to report there wasn't much perishable food, or not much that hadn't already perished completely.

I remember the moment in the dark gray light at the end of the day, as we finally tied up the mouths of the black garbage bags, when I knew Harris would ask me to lie down with him.

That night I lay down with Harris and he held me. I counted to five and got up and went to the sofa, and on that night we became brother and sister.

●

I stood right in front of a boy with a white guitar at a house concert in a Massachusetts town before I was twenty. He played his guitar and looked down at his fingers and looked out at the room and didn't look at me. He gave me the gift of being allowed my longing. I needed to enjoy it, to suffer it, as I did.

Lust howled in me. It howls everywhere, that delighted rage. It was like that, what the boy with the white guitar did for me.

It is a comfort to know that the other will always love you more than you love him. If it continues long enough, something peculiar happens—you start to love the other more for loving you more.

Then, when he dies, you'll wonder how his death could have burned you entirely away—yet there you are, walking out of the fire in a form you no longer recognize.

•

Lost in California, driving fast, Harris called me in Brooklyn and asked me to navigate him west, out of Riverside County. As in the old story, the wanderer hears a disembodied voice that leads him out of the desert.

It worked so well that for months afterward, whenever he was lost, he called me. It was always nighttime in New York, and I'd look at a road atlas under my desk light and tell him what was there.

•

Harris's sister writes, *You were indeed one of his closest friends. Almost like a sister, really. I should know! I once asked him why you guys never dated and among many mumbled excuses, he said he didn't want to disturb anything.*

His mother writes, *I cannot begin to express the depth of Harris's feelings for you.*

Everyone else writes, *What are you working on?*

I'm working on a book about a man who jumps in front of a train. I have no interest in hanging a true story on an artificial scaffolding of plot, but what is the true story? My friend died—that isn't a story.

•

Harris painted some canvas boards with black line segments at right angles and colored in some of the areas red and yellow and blue. In the right light he had a pretty good collection of Mondrians.

When splitting a bill with a group of three or more, he always threw in a dollar or two less than the rest of us.

He forgot to flush the toilet when someone's mother was visiting.

He was concerned that he possessed a one-way refrigerator. He said, *The thing is, I keep putting food into it, and then I forget about it and by the time I remember it, the food's gone bad. It's starting to cost money. Does your refrigerator have this problem?* I told him my refrigerator was a two-way, that I hadn't paid extra for it, but that he should specify to his next landlord that he would need a two-way refrigerator. This conversation is approximate. Imagine having it with a mental patient.

Now imagine having it with a regular person, your friend, on the sunniest afternoon in the world.

After you have seen someone play the fiddle like a devil, it is hard to tell the devil to stop humming into his kasha while you try to have a nice dinner, particularly if he has been a reasonable participant in conversations for seven years or so.

The devil took and ruined the thing that made my friend brilliant.

Harris's front teeth ground against each other and got shorter. Music possessed him. He hummed and whistled and sang and jerked his head and ground his teeth. He did it quietly, but it was never invisible. He had to do it.

It came and went, the devil inside him. When it was gone, I wished it would never come back, and when it came back, I blamed Harris.

•

Far away in California, Harris had stayed up very late with friends, and he thought someone had laced his drink with a hallucinogen, but when he was admitted to the psychiatric ward, he reported having taken something on purpose.

By the time he'd been released from the hospital, he felt quite sure he hadn't meant to take anything. He tried to remember the order of events leading to his hospitalization, but he was unsure of too many details, and it's hard to remember a story about someone else's confusion.

.

Harris called one day to ask whether he should clean his toilet seat or just buy a new one. I told him to clean the old one, described with agitation a vision of a land-fill occupied only by toilet seats, their owners having thrown them away rather than cleaning them, a moun-tain of cream-colored plastic rings flecked with dark yellow. I don't know if he ever cleaned it. Why do I re-member this?

.

The dictionary defines psychosis as *the abnormal condition of the mind*, which doesn't narrow it down much.

The clinical definition narrows it down to *a loss of contact with reality*, but how does one make contact with an abstraction?

The diagnosis depends on the report of a person whose reports are, by clinical definition, unreliable. Hallucina-tions and delusional beliefs may accompany unusual or bizarre behavior, difficulty with social interaction, and impairment in carrying out daily life activities.

There's nothing to measure, just judgments of what

is *unusual or bizarre*, what constitutes *difficulty and impairment*.

Another of my friends was eight years old when his father abandoned the family, draining his three sons' college funds, leaving them bankrupt. For weeks afterward, my tiny friend hallucinated in his second-grade classroom, hearing voices that told him terrible things were coming.

The dimensional approach to defining psychosis argues that full-blown psychotic illness is just the most extreme end of the schizotypy spectrum. The dimensional approach makes sense to me. My comrades in lockdown were the same as those I knew outside lockdown, but just a bit more overcome by sadness or confusion or fear.

The distinctions between us and those suffering from psychosis may be whittled down to nothing, but the fact stands that we fear being what they are, fear seeing what they see, fear knowing what they know, and so we believe they are different, and so it is so.

•

In the last eleven years, I've taken many psychotropic medications and had very many side effects, some of them almost unbelievably strange. One of them, dyskinesia— often characterized by repetitive, involuntary, purposeless movements, such as grimacing, tongue protrusion, lip smacking, puckering and pursing of the lips—is a common side effect of long-term use of antipsychotic medication.

For the last few months of the four years I spent on olanzapine, whenever I lied or said anything even slightly insincere, my right shoulder jerked up and my head jerked down to meet it. At a dinner party, even if I agreed with someone that I too had liked a book that I hadn't really liked, my body would make those same involuntary movements. I couldn't lie even a little, or my shoulder would try to give me away.

I'm so glad to see you, I'd say to someone I loathed, and up went the shoulder. I was good enough at incorporating the involuntary movement into the regular, casual movements of my body that people swore they didn't notice, but after months passed, and the symptom stayed, I traded olanzapine for quetiapine, and my shoulder stayed down.

Antipsychotics bring the risk of a variety of weird side effects. Impaired spatial orientation. Impaired responses to senses. Akathisia, which is harder to explain because the words used to describe its subjective experience are uselessly abstract: *torment, restlessness, pulling or drawing or twisting sensations, a desire to move, a difficulty in staying still.*

The word was coined by a Czech doctor, Ladislav Haškovec, in a French medical journal in 1901. Its objective indicators are perversely indistinguishable from those of anxiety. Haškovec reported two cases of a curious movement disorder. In one case,

the patient's gait was normal, but as soon as he sat down, he would start jumping as if he were on horseback. For two weeks, he also experienced "pins and needles" in his fingers, and for a shorter period felt a twisting movement in his mouth. When forced to sit down, he would suddenly jump, and then regain his seat. His movements seemed automatic, involuntary, driven, and the patient experienced them as such.

In the other case,

the patient could not remain sitting down for any length of time. Upon doing so, he would violently jump in the air. The same occurred regardless of whether he was on his own or in a public place. He sometimes had to hang on to the table so as to stop himself from jumping up. When he was able to sit down, he still had the sensation that he was jumping in the air.

Haškovec wrote, *If the phenomenon in question proves to be common . . . it can be suggested that it is called* akathisia *(α, privative + καθίζω, sitting).*

•

The phenomenon Haškovec called *akathisia* had been recorded anecdotally for a long time—in fact, one of the chamberlains of Napoleon III suffered from severe restlessness of the legs, and when in court, and even in the presence of the emperor, he had to walk around every few minutes.

Akathisia became clinically relevant in the 1950s, when the first high-potency antipsychotic medication was discovered. The condition seemed to result more frequently at higher doses. Some studies now show upwards of 75 percent of patients suffering akathisia with clinical doses. *Extraordinary suffering. Intolerable restlessness. Unbearable discomfort.* These are the words the journals use.

Second-generation antipsychotics, which had less risk of extrapyramidal side effects—those related to the neural network in the brain involved in the coordination of movement—were introduced in the 1990s and have begun to replace first-generation antipsychotics.

Akathisia still exists, though. By now it's a recognized side effect of antipsychotic drugs as well as antiemetic drugs once used as antipsychotics. It's possible that some people are more prone to it than others.

The phenomenon is recognized, but it can be difficult to diagnose when symptoms develop gradually or without adequate clinical supervision. Patients often find it difficult to explain in words, and as a result it's easily misinterpreted as acute anxiety, depression, psychosis, agitation, mania, terror, or anger.

If there were a way to describe the experience of this disorder more clearly, clinicians might better be able to diagnose it, treat it, and prevent its common outcomes, which in the literature are overwhelmingly identified as homicide and suicide—specifically by jumping.

•

There are hours of recordings that I can't listen to, in which Harris speaks, laughs, and plays music, and there are six hundred and fifty photographs. My favorite ones depict Harris playing the violin—not because of his obvious joy but because of the way his hands hold the instrument. They were competent hands. The bow and the body of the instrument were obedient to them. Everything else I can say about the way he played music is the regular sort of thing. The music he played was good. The feeling he showed was delight in what was good.

The person who sat with a famous musician as he

died reported that his last words were *I can hear the music all around me.*

On Harris's thirtieth birthday, he beams so brightly he looks uncomfortable, as if the joy needs some greater outlet than his mouth, his eyes, his face. Everyone he knows stands around him.

In the photographs from the last year of his life, his face looks doughier than I remember it. His eyes focus on something very far away. The month before he died, he was photographed drinking coffee, wearing a blue shirt, and squinting into the sun.

It is impossible not to read the photographs as summaries: Harris drinks coffee now because he is trying to waken from a terrible dream; Harris wears blue because it suggests heavenly grace; Harris squints at the bright light of the next world, at the headlight on the diesel locomotive.

•

I moved to Italy for a year and fell out of contact with my friends back home. From time to time I spoke with an editor of some publication or other. No one visited. I spent most of my time in my studio, avoiding the receptions and the teas, and developed an eye twitch, migraines, and eczema.

On my way to the hallway bathroom I always ran

into someone who would greet me with some well-meaning banality that wrapped me in frustrated loathing and prevented me from writing for the rest of the day.

One day I took an expensive trip—two cabs, two trains, and a funicular—all for a little lasagna on a terrace and a stroll through a medieval town, even though all of Tuscany and Umbria looks the same to me. I spent the day walking around half numb, wishing I were in my studio, working.

During my travels I dutifully described in my little notebook all the things I saw in Paris, Barcelona, Valletta, Stuttgart, Vienna, Naples. Afterward none of the descriptions interested me.

A linguist told me serenely that when writers go mad, they go mad in interesting ways, but the rash on my eyelids was not interesting. I scratched at it and smeared cream on it for months, knowing it would make the skin weaker, the rash worse. The symbolic ruination of my eyes was wretchedly trite. I visited new cities and towns and collected descriptions of all there was to see. I never reread them.

Instead of transcribing my travel journals I spent most of my fellowship year trying and failing to write a novel about a research prison where people are monitored invisibly until they go insane. I went a little mad, up in my cell in the villa on the highest hill in Rome. After dinner I often walked down into the cryptoporticus, lifted the heavy trapdoor, and descended the ladder into the first-century aqueduct, which was always quiet, damp, and cool.

The others sat in the living room amid tapestries, eating cookies and fruit, discussing engravings and the sites in the country where stones used to be.

•

I went to a psychiatrist who lived and practiced a few blocks from Vatican City.

His eyelids were blankets on an unmade bed, his eyes hidden. He was tiny, ancient, and known in his field for a study he'd published in the 1950s. His half-grown-out red-dyed hair looked satanic. At our first meeting he wrote down everything I said. At our second meeting, after he told me his hourly rate, I immediately apologized and said I wouldn't be able to return. *Clever girl!* he sneered.

Eventually I sent him a cashier's check via certified mail, which in Rome is approximately a weeklong errand. Hundreds of euros later, I was adrift in a foreign country for a year with no doctor and three empty pill vials.

The pharmacists on Via Carini, bless them, tried to take care of me.

•

After a month in Rome I went to the Great Synagogue for the Kol Nidre service, the holiest of the Jewish year. I went with a new friend, one of the only Jews in town I knew.

At the first checkpoint we were frisked. The Italian sneered at my friend's Israeli passport, *Non vuol dire un cazzo qui.* (*That doesn't mean dick here.*) At the second checkpoint we were interrogated in English. *Are you Jewish? Is he your husband? Why are you here together? Why are you in Rome?*

We moved past the second checkpoint and my friend entered the synagogue. I entered through a side door and climbed a lot of stairs. The balcony was half-filled with chattering women. They held prayer books on their laps but didn't look down.

From the fourth balcony row I could see the men downstairs in their shawls, davening, could hear the low echo of their prayer. The prayer book was in Hebrew and Italian, and I was illiterate in both, neither sufficiently Jewish nor sufficiently Italian. A woman dressed in a shabby turtleneck sweater and jeans and a dirty dress greeted me in English. I turned to her, wounded. *How did you know?*

Well, I speak only English and Hebrew, and it's unlikely

anyone in Rome speaks Hebrew. She was from Israel, in Rome on vacation. While she and I tried to make small talk, another woman laid a blue scarf over my knees, scolded me in a language I didn't understand. I was dressed in my one black suit with a skirt that showed my knee-caps when I sat. The scarf might as well have been an American flag.

The Israeli woman leaned over the railing and followed the service, beating her chest at the right moments.

A Roman woman addressed me in English and smiled at my question. She said, *I can tell you are a stranger.* She meant that I was foreign, *una straniera.*

After half-believing all my life that if I ever went to Italy I would immediately become Italian, that my name would anchor me there, that the word *Manguso* would radiate from me in a language transcending language, I understood then that no Italian would ever think I looked Italian.

Weeks later I learned that outside Sicily, my Sicilian name *non vuol dire un cazzo.*

•

I went to France and found Paris's slowness grand, languorous, not lazy like Rome's maddening crawl. On the Left Bank I passed a table of used books—all color,

clothbound books about animals except for one, a history
of the Jews.

I am aware of accuracy as an abstract goal, but I don't
know what it looks like or how to find it or how I would
know it if I found it or what I would do if I did.

•

The man who wasn't yet my husband and I went to
Malta. I'd been invited to give a talk at the university
for American Culture Week.

We registered in the hotel as Mr. and Mrs. Manguso.
Since we knew Catholicism was the country's state reli-
gion, we didn't correct the register to reflect that we were
in fact an unmarried man and his Jewish companion.

Later in the week, when we asked a woman at the
university what percentage of the country was Catholic,
she assured us that only about 90 percent of the country
attend mass regularly.

In fact, 98 percent of the population identifies as Roman Catholic, and according to the most recent census,
there are twenty-five Jewish families in the entire country, most of them elderly. When a male child is born to one
of the twenty-five families, a mohel is flown in from Italy
to perform the bris.

In those last few months before the euro became
the official currency, coffee cost seven cents, a pea-filled

pastizz cost eleven cents, an expensive dinner a few Maltese lire. The signs on the buildings were Victorian relics—*House Furnisher. Gilders. General Store, Est. 1828.* The key to our hotel room was a large iron five-lever item that could have been a theater prop.

After I ate bad fish and swelled up and my face turned purple, and we watched the purple tinge creep slowly down my chest, the man who wasn't yet my husband ran downstairs to the concierge and said the first thing that occurred to him—*My wife is ill.*

A doctor was summoned. He gave me a shot in the arm that cost twenty-five lire. The purple faded. Then I got dressed and went to the university and gave my talk.

That was the first time my husband ever called me *wife.*

•

In the novel I failed to write in Rome, the protagonist writes in his journal,

> The historian walked the halls like a young war hero. Since the first time we met he hailed me in the same way, the inflection unvarying. His head turned toward me in a rictus of courtesy. If I saw him in the morning, that day's work was ruined.

When I arose early I found him in the laundry room ironing a pile of shirts, with a perfectly shaven neck, standing upright as a soldier. He stood for hours in handsome alignment, one arm moving back and forth over the hateful stripes.

The hallway greetings were shouted out, the faces turned toward each other, then away, the atoms of scent hanging in the air as human debris collected on the wine-colored carpet runner, miasmic clouds hovering like devil-masks, and I wondered at the contentment of the historian to contain nothing, mean nothing, say nothing, show nothing, be nothing.

Instead of working on the Anagram Notebooks now I spend the days writing lines of script and then blacking out parts of them. The pages need to be rewritten and re-blacked and rewritten and re-blacked many more times, but there is always more to remember and more to write.

•

The man who wasn't yet my husband spent weeks visiting the Fascist-constructed suburb Esposizione Universale Roma, or EUR, pronounced *ehh-urr*, at dusk each day, in order to take visual records of the swarms of European starlings, which assemble an hour before sunset to dance in the sky.

He stood for hours under an umbrella, a million and a half sphincterless animals flying above his camera and his head. They fill the sky with pointillist accumulations— rotating funnels, whipping sails, dense black stones. It might mean something, if we could read what they write on the blue page of the sky. They could be avoiding hungry raptors, strengthening flock bonds, warming their bodies, maneuvering for roost position, or celebrating. We don't know why they do it.

•

All year in Rome, I missed my real life so much, I couldn't bring myself to visit or to write home more than a few lines. I dreamt I was still there.

Then, after a year, the dream was real.

I wept in New York City subway cars in gratitude for their languages, their music, and their people's benign tolerance. The city swelled hot with love. It was summer. Everything would be the same as before, except that now I would appreciate every sandwich, every good song I heard on a train platform.

During my first week at home I ate my last little sack of a particular candy I ate all through the year in Rome and only ever found at one candy shop, Confetteria

Moriondo e Gariglio—tiny cordial drops, candy spheres the size of currants, filled with sweet liquor in two dozen colors and flavors: blueberry, violet, grape, almond, honeydew, banana, rose, anise. I am told the liquor has to be hand-dropped onto starch, and that they are impossible to mass-produce.

They were always displayed in an arrogant pastel heap on a footed glass dish. If one of them broke and spilled its liquor, the entire pile would be ruined. That's how perfectly they were made.

They are called *lacrime d'amore*, tears of love.

.

On my ninth day home from Rome, I was told Harris had disappeared, that he'd already been gone three days. I hadn't spoken with him in a year.

He had run away—*eloped*, as it's said—from a hospital and left his wallet, keys, and cell phone. The police had begun a search. I hadn't seen him since I'd come home. I couldn't remember the last time I'd seen him before I'd gone away. It seemed like a puzzle on the back page of a magazine, absolutely separate from the real New York, where Harris lay in his apartment sleeping, waiting until morning to call me.

Where's Harris? He's somewhere on that back page, hiding in a crowd of Harrises, walking among them,

Harrises all over the Brooklyn Bridge in bright sun. It's just a game. I could throw away the magazine, the puzzle left unsolved, and it wouldn't matter.

I spent the day getting used to the idea that Harris had disappeared from the real New York, that he might have gone where no one would ever find him. One day wasn't enough time to get used to the idea that he might be absolutely gone. I was still reattaching myself to the city, relocating myself in the crowd of it. I felt as if time itself had made a mistake. The disappearance seemed not so much impossible as just wrong.

The next morning, just before I learned Harris was dead, the man who wasn't yet my husband lay sleeping next to me. I watched him until I could no longer wait, and then I woke him and said, *Harris was committed again but he's been missing for three days and I'm afraid he's dead.*

I wasn't afraid until I said it.

•

On the day the body was identified, everyone who knew about the death gathered in one house. Someone phoned to tell me the address. I didn't know who lived there, but I went. I asked the woman who answered the door, *What was your connection to Harris?* and she answered, *Love.*

The floor was thick with green trimmings. Everyone was crying or had just cried or was about to cry, but

Jonathan the software programmer, Harris's colleague from long ago, cried unceasingly. Who was this inconsolable Jonathan?

It was July. The kitchen smelled of old milk. Somewhere in the old house was a table where a perfect Manhattan stood in a tumbler collecting sweat.

Back in the room of growth and death, flowers and rot, we cried, then stopped crying, then started again. People baked cake after cake. I washed every dish I saw, pacing myself so I never had to stop.

The oven floated a hot smell around us, a sweet miasma.

The scene goes on. Someone brings more flour, more butter, more milk, more flowers, while Jonathan cries. The leafy mat underneath us rises as the cakes rise. An enormous garden throbs outside the back door of the house. We bring the cakes to the people there. We are the people there. We bring stems and long leaves to the people in the kitchen, and we add them to the vases and the floor.

We tread slowly on the grass, tread slowly on the green, far beyond, far beyond, far beyond.

•

Harris might have become manic on the ward, convinced the doctors were trying to kill him.

He might have jumped a subway turnstile.

He might have walked, in pouring rain, to the Bronx.

He might have thought he was saving himself from something.

He wandered for ten hours before getting in front of a bright light in Riverdale.

It doesn't matter if he thought of me, wanted to call me, missed me, felt angry at me, loved me, but it's impossible not to invite oneself into the black box of a forsaken mind.

It must be very beautiful to be finished. When the train rushes into the station, to let the wind blow into your face. Suppose your whole life surges back to you. I try to believe that Harris summoned all the beauty of his life.

I'm comforted when I remember that energy that appears missing has just gone somewhere else, has been surrendered to the system of the world.

•

I thought I would write ravishingly about the last ten hours of Harris's life. I'd make it into a story—a man walks out of a building and eats a whitefish sandwich and gets a little fish oil on his hands and rubs it into the skin, conditioning it, seasoning it, remembering that what we clean from ourselves is not always unwelcome.

His hands redolent of fish, he walks outside without

an umbrella—at this moment I am reminded of my landlord who said to me, after his liver transplant, on a rainy day, with perfect hatred, *I have never carried an umbrella in my life.* The rain falls on him hard.

Harris looks at the old buildings and knows they will outlast him. He looks at the clothes and the fruits displayed under awnings and behind vitrines and knows they will outlast him like the sky, the sun, the material of the clouds.

His hair is thin on top and his scalp is very white. His expensive eyeglasses are dirty. He taps rhythms on his hips and thighs as he walks, whistling and humming a little, grinding syncopations with his tea-stained teeth.

He walks west into the park, finds a ledge that will protect something the size and shape of his body. The rain falls lighter now, and he is cold from sitting still. He extricates his body from what it has crouched under, and he walks east again to the avenue, or west across the park, and at some point, down to the subterranean train that takes him across the body of water dividing Manhattan from Queens, and he sits whistling and is ejected from the train.

He sits on a bench at the track for three hours after the sun sets. The lights keep him from feeling completely alone, for he can see the forms of the others on the platform and in the station.

He is still whistling a little, the music in his head unabating, both punishment and balm. Trains come and go on the far track and the near track.

He stands as if ready to deliver something.

The sound of the train approaches, the light of its light in the wet dark, maybe a veil of mist now between him and it. He walks across the platform to the yellow edge. Maybe he thinks about the way his body looks, how it would look to someone looking at it. Maybe he is looking at it.

During the next moment he's alive, and during the moment after that he isn't alive yet still exists, just not anymore as himself but as a body thrown in front of a train, which raises the questions of responsibility and blame.

Did Harris throw someone's body under a train?

If I could I would blame him, but I can identify Harris only with the body, not with the one who threw the body.

•

Late for some concert, when we arrived on a crowded subway platform, Harris said, *A platform filled with people— that's what I like to see.*

Since then, whenever I find a crowded platform, I remember what he said and feel glad. Soon the train will come! Despite everything, I'm always happy on a crowded platform.

I wish I could pretend the last minute of Harris's life wasn't ruined by fear. Isn't the mind supposed to degrade memory into more manageable forms, to contaminate it with false memories we'd prefer to the real ones?

This is what I'm trying to remember instead: *A train comes, and my friend is on it. He waves to me. I grin from the platform. People look at us and wonder if they should remember it. And that train takes him away forever.*

•

At the memorial three months after Harris's funeral, his last lover was beautiful and calm, and all through it I thought it was easy for her because she'd known him only a few months, less than a year.

She kept her distance, and I understood. She had been the last one to go to bed with Harris. At least she had that. Maybe she didn't want that last intimacy threatened by someone who had known her lover ten times longer than she had. I didn't want my own intimacy threatened by hers.

How can intimacy be threatened? It isn't a finite substance like gold or coal, a friend chides. But of course it is, and I missed the whole last year of it, and now there isn't any of it left.

•

I picked up some earth in the shovel and let it fall onto the casket. I'm glad I remember the sound of it.

A Catholic asked me about the raging and the yelling and the weeping at Harris's funeral, having never seen it before. *It's because for Jews, death is real*, I told her, understanding it myself for the first time, the reason I prefer Jewish funerals to Catholic ones, where we're told that heaven waits for us happily, with all its lights on.

•

One week after the funeral, Harris's sister cleaned out his apartment. Harris's two oldest friends went along. His parents didn't. They said I should go to help sort Harris's things, to take whatever I wanted to remember him by—furniture, books, whatever was there, but I couldn't, wouldn't, go.

I didn't want anything to remember Harris by and I didn't want to see his hair on the bathroom floor or smell the breath trapped in his bedclothes or see what books he had read or what food he had left in the refrigerator. I didn't want to know any of that. I had just returned from a year away, and I hadn't seen Harris yet, and I wanted to hold on to that word, *yet*.

I'd helped Harris move into that place a couple of

years before. I'd told him not to take his grandmother's enormous oak wardrobe, that the closet and a dresser would suffice, but he wouldn't listen. The thing looked like a coffin.

Harris's two oldest friends dragged trash onto the street and lifted the wardrobe into a truck and took Harris's bookends and his tea mugs and his salt and pepper shakers.

There was one thing I wouldn't have minded having—a literary journal I'd signed and given to Harris because it contained a poem I'd written for him, about him. One of the lines is *Winnie, I am writing this on behalf of my friend Harris. He loves you and wants you to love him.* Harris's sister told me she wanted me to have it, but when I asked her about it months later, she said she'd decided to keep it, and I realized I didn't need it.

•

One of the men who helped clear out Harris's apartment—a better, braver friend—told me someone had broken into the place weeks earlier, while Harris was still alive.

The place wasn't dirty, but . . .

Dark gray inky fingerprints dotted the white laminate surface of a credenza. Harris hadn't cleaned up the mess from the forensic work. The police had tried to find the remnants of a story no one was there to see, and the artifact of their attempt to find the story outlasted the story.

It felt exhilarating. We were a team. We were on a mission.

There were musical instruments—accordions, violins, and mandolins, including the solid-body one Harris had made. There were screws, bolts, nails, rolls of paper towels.

All those paper towels—he wasn't planning on being dead.

There were three vacuum cleaners.

I took one of them. Now it's the Harris J. Wulfson Memorial Vacuum Cleaner.

Was the bed made?

I think his bed was made.

He was the first person I ever knew who read the paper in bed on a laptop.

We kept bringing things out to the street, and people kept taking them. We went to his office and asked to speak with someone in Human Resources, and when we told the man Harris was dead, he burst into tears.

•

Three months after Harris's funeral, I didn't go to the memorial concert his other friends had prepared because I wasn't going to continue without Harris. Everyone else could mourn, obedient, but I would not participate.

I'm raising the tiny irrational child of Harris's death. It hides, then appears and demands all my attention and all my power. I limit its range: When I teach, I will not think of it; when I run, I will not think of it; when I am with others, I will not think of it. But then it surprises me and I have to go home and be with it, tend to it.

I take good care of the little infant death. It's learning to behave.

I don't think I can live without Harris, I tell it.

You'd be surprised by what you can live without, it tells me.

•

At some point I stopped believing that Harris died when the train touched his body and started believing that he died when he walked through the door of the unlocked ward, as if his life ended on the far side of the threshold, as if the ten last hours of his life didn't happen, but they did.

He walked or ran or sat or stood or ate or spoke or touched something or someone. He walked or ran or rode in a car or a train from Manhattan to the Bronx for ten hours during which someone might have found him and saved him by putting him back on the other side of the door but didn't.

In ten hours you can work a full shift, eat lunch, and drive home. In ten hours Jupiter and Saturn rotate approximately once. New York to Pittsburgh takes ten hours by bus. Los Angeles to London takes ten hours by plane.

The ten missing hours would make a good story if I liked making up stories, but I don't. I try not to make anything up, and I fail every time.

•

For the first year I thought I'd wait until I'd really adjusted to the loss, maybe wait ten years. Now it's been less than two years and I wish I'd started writing ten years ago. Preparing, writing down all the things Harris and I ever said to each other.

While composing my eulogy, I could remember only a few things, among them the lines from a movie that we'd recite to each other after one of us had a bad experience in love. One of us would ask, *What makes you so happy?* And then the other would say the woman's line, *Well, I'm very shallow and empty and I have no ideas and nothing interesting to say*, and then the other would say the man's line, *And I'm exactly the same way.*

When I recited the lines during my eulogy, everyone laughed.

•

Statistics show that suicides increase until people reach their mid-forties, after which they subside until people reach their mid-eighties. Maybe the idea of middle age is what makes people kill themselves. *If I'm only halfway there*, a forty-two-year-old thinks—

If this is it, an eighty-four-year-old thinks—

When a poet ends her life, ghouls send lines of the dead woman's poems back and forth all day. Everyone wants to find the most prescient, the most declaratory statement that she would always have done it, that we would never have been able to prevent it. Or maybe we want to find a clue we should have noticed, since it was right there in her poems, all along, that we should have known to save her, that she had wanted us to.

I remember taking the train out of the city with her, eating lunch with her, listening to her and perceiving her frizzy cloud of hair as an extension of the tightly wound spring of her mind. We visited a roomful of graduate students and read from our books, answered a few questions, then went home separately. I haven't thought about her in seven years, but all day I go online to find the lines people have extracted from her books. All day long I read her poems.

In one of them, she wrote: *How many mourners can fill a hall? / Room for them all.*

•

I read the obituaries every day to learn what sorts of lives are available to us, to see an entire life compressed into a few column inches, to fit the whole story in my eye at once.

I say I'm interested in life, but really I want to play a little game with Death. I want to lie down next to him and smell his infected breath.

After he pins me with his rotten arms and burst knees, gray bone showing at the joint, I want to wake up alone with bruised eyes, his hair in my teeth. And then I want to whisper a little story about him inside the safest locked room in the world.

·

In the church of Saint Mary in Rome's Piazza del Popolo hang two paintings by Caravaggio. The one depicting the conversion of Saint Paul was finished in 1601, the year Shakespeare finished *Hamlet*.

It seems a remarkable coincidence until I consider all the other things from 1601 that are gone, all the people who walked on the stones of the piazza before me—I feel them surging through it, four hundred years in a moment—absolutely gone. All the pretty girls and boys who left behind nothing but flesh, the flesh of their flesh, which is gone but for the flesh of its flesh, and so on.

·

My journal from the day I met my husband reads, *Beat the tall man at pool.*

The next day reads, *He laughs loudly at the things I say and swears when he loses at pool—twice more today.*

The next day reads, *I like people who possess either deep mastery or deep empathy, but not as much as I like those who possess both.*

Three weeks later, not knowing anything about it, an ex-lover proposed to me in a letter, and I realized I was already married.

·

Like everyone from Hawaii, where ghosts are integral, my husband knows people who have seen them, and he knows that the ghosts are preceded on their path by ghost dogs, and that if one sees the dogs or senses their approach, one is to look away, as the ghosts are not to be regarded by the living.

Harris stayed near me for about two months after I was married. I didn't see him, but he was there. By then he had been dead almost a year. Then one day he was gone.

He was gone, but in Texas, during a business trip, my husband woke in the night to find a ghost—a man in a broad-brimmed hat standing in the corner of the room. Though I am dubious of ghosts who are said to appear in human form, I considered that it might have been Harris, gone to Texas to watch my husband for me, to keep him safe and to remind him to be faithful.

I consulted the photographic archive assembled by his friends but found no photograph of Harris in a broad-brimmed hat. I did, however, find a photograph of me placing a white-frosted cake before him on the night of his twentieth birthday. He exhales carefully onto the candles. I don't remember it—it may as well have happened to someone else.

·

At first I thought a death was a thing in itself, a discrete item in the world, a piece of time and space.

When I asked an elite runner why he started going long distances, he said, *It was part of a larger pattern.*

At first I thought a marriage was a thing in itself, a discrete item in the world.

My husband and I invited six friends to our courthouse ceremony. When it was over, he and I went to the beach for a week. At the seaside cabin we tried to do nothing but be married, but by the third day we both mourned that we'd had to leave our work aside per the honeymoon convention.

On our fourth day at the cabin we declared the week a *working honeymoon* and for the rest of the day I wrote sentences and he made drawings, together but silent, against the background of the sea. The cabin was so remote that deer walked by, their hooves crunching the sea pebbles. Rabbits and moles emerged from the bramble.

At night my husband and I ate fresh fish and walked on the sand and told each other what we'd made that day.

•

Three weeks after the vows we had a party at a little restaurant near our apartment. People came from out of town. After it was over, I put on flat shoes and walked home with my husband.

Weeks or months after the party, having failed to find a suitable answer to my question among the living, I asked Harris if I should change my name. He had been dead a year. He answered, *Not right away.*

•

My poem for Harris is a persuasive address to a woman he loved. It's a poem about what young people care about—falling in love, getting the girl, starting something.

When people aren't young anymore, they care about other things, sustaining love, and whether, a long time from now, things will be the same or different, and whether the beloved will be the same or different, or maybe when people begin to care more about those things than about starting something, that tendency is what makes them stop being young.

Marriage helped me forget my potential, helped me learn to attend to the present moment. During our first year together, after every quarrel, my husband and I examined and speculated on the relationships of people we knew, describing lovingly to each other their myriad flaws. Now we're almost able to see our own.

•

Exactly one year after Harris's funeral, on the elevated track the wrong train screamed murderously by and didn't stop. I waited at the outer track for the local, wanting to sob, my husband beside me. The train to the unveiling was five minutes, fifteen minutes, twenty-five minutes late.

I felt myself standing very straight and still, in my one black suit, relying on my posture to keep me calm. Then I remembered I was on my way to Harris's unveiling, and I sobbed downstairs to the street and hailed a cab, and my husband and I rode it to Long Island and gave eighty dollars to the driver when we got out at the

Jewish cemetery where my friend's body had disintegrated for a year.

What I find most interesting is that the train did stop, of course, at the appointed time, but I so faithfully believed what was written on the misprinted schedule, I didn't see it stop, didn't for a moment believe I could possibly be in the wrong place.

·

We went back to the spot in the earth just above where Harris's body is buried. The granite headstone stood with a white linen sash covering part of his name.

There isn't just one unveiling. Every moment is the unveiling of the preceding moment. We might as well take the veils for granted, ignore them as we ignore air, dust, the passage of time.

The granite headstone stood under bright sun. We stood in a ring around it. The grandmother sat in a folding chair. She was ninety-one that year.

The rabbi spoke, sighed, used the full range of his voice. We knew Harris was dead. We'd known it all year. Then the rabbi removed the sash and made it real for us, and we thanked him. I dutifully cried.

The mourning over, the grandmother held my hand and said, *We must move past this. We must.* Her words sounded banal to my ear, but in that I am interested in how people live to be ninety-one, I noted them. It's possible they are very important.

•

The night after Harris's unveiling, I turned on the television.

The protagonist sits at his writing desk in the eighteenth century, hears a knock at the door, opens it to find a man with dirt in his hair and blood on his face. There has been a terrible impact between something and his body, and when I saw this beaten man I thought it was Harris.

My dead friend was on television, made up to look beaten. I screamed and turned off the television. I couldn't bear even the suggestion that he might have lived through the impact with the train. In fact, I couldn't bear to think that he ever had been alive, that he ever wasn't dead. As far as my mind was concerned, at all possible points in time, my friend was a dead man.

•

I still see Harris everywhere.

I know it isn't him, but when I see someone who resembles him I stare, take in as much information as possible, knowing that in a moment he'll stop being Harris, that he'll turn back into someone else.

When I find a substitute Harris I always think of my friend's cat, Roy, who loved playing with the laser pointer. My friend would hand me the device and say *He knows it's fake but he loves it anyway,* and I'd send the pink laser-dot over the rug, the floor, the vertical front of the sofa, and Roy would slap away at it, trying to pin it with his soft orange paw.

•

Don't tell me about the rich variety of mourning customs throughout the world from the beginning of civilizations to now—I don't want to know about customs. I don't care to know how others act out the playlet of their ruination.

I want to know about my particular grief, which is unknowable, just like everyone else's.

•

I knew a woman who spent years mourning a dead friend. She threw away all her clothes and dressed all in black, then threw away her black clothes and dressed all in white. She took elaborate detours so she wouldn't ever walk past a restaurant where she'd eaten with her friend. She stopped eating certain foods, went to church every Sunday and prayed secret prayers but never took communion, dedicated hours and days to her grief. From my vantage point it resembled a child's game, an idle person's dream of purpose and utility.

The feeling of love isn't for the beloved. It's for the lover. When people tell me they feel breathless with love, I don't care. Their breathlessness is for them. Only their behavior toward the beloved counts. Only behavior shows love, is love.

That's why I'm ashamed of my grief.

During the first year, my job was to comfort Harris's family and friends, to comfort and care for myself so I could help the others. Shiva is a social responsibility. But my grieving past shiva isn't for the parents, who must relearn to care for each other instead of their dead son, and my grief isn't for Harris. My grief is for myself.

•

Sometimes I try to believe that while I was away for a year, Harris gradually faded away, achieved greater understanding, passed on to the life triumphant, and that I missed the yearlong process—that his gait slowed and the flesh on his face thinned, that he started sleeping more, turned up the morphine drip, and so on.

Death has been presented to me so many times, in movies and photographs and writing and life, always the same—the gradual fading of a person in a bed, swathed in white, a slow, clean, elegant fade.

None of those things happened to Harris. He had an experience unknowable to anyone but him, an *episode*, and then was well again, and then had another episode, and then was well again, and then had another one, during which something happened and he died.

Those who have had one seizure are from then on cared for as if always on the verge of another seizure. If I were capable of anything beyond contemplation and record, I'd devise a maintenance protocol for those diagnosed with episodic psychotic illness. I'd devise a simple instruction that everyone in the world would learn—*Stop, drop, and roll! Thrust the fist under the rib cage! Pinch the nose and blow into the mouth!*—and from that point on, those vulnerable to future psychotic breaks would be safer.

Then again, the protocol for those suffering florid psychosis, as Harris was at the time of his third hospitalization, is to lock them in and guard them.

My friend didn't die of some secret tumor. He died because someone opened the door of a building. I imagine telling him that.

He would have said *Oh, Sarah.*

•

When my husband and I moved to Los Angeles from New York, I unpacked everything right away. I don't like traveling. I like staying home. I love unpacking most of all.

Wedged between the tape and the cardboard of one of my boxes was a man's wedding band, silver, engraved. I'd never seen it. It had to belong to one of the men who'd moved the boxes into or out of a truck, so I wrote a letter to the moving company with a photograph of the ring, assuming that one of the men had been looking for it.

No one wrote back. I called. I found the name of the foreman who had packed everything. I left him a message. No one called back, no one wrote back. I keep the ring buried in a bowl of seashells so I don't have to look at it. I'm quite sure my husband has forgotten about it.

I'm in denial not that I've moved to Los Angeles, but that I've left New York. Somehow my mind has convinced me that I'll just be living in both places now, with all my friends and everything the same, but with a few additional things, like palm trees, freeways, and sun.

I'm in denial not that Harris is dead, but that he isn't alive.

•

The worth of a single man's life in New York State is a few hundred thousand dollars.

Harris's sister told me she'd refuse to be involved in any legal proceedings, if there ever were any.

Harris's parents gave me permission to write this book and dedicated a bench to him in Prospect Park. After a plaque was attached to the bench, and the first group of Harris's friends went to visit it, one of them told me it was twenty feet away from where it was supposed to be.

Five people picked it up and carried it back to the appropriate tree.

In Memory of
Harris J. Wulfson
1974–2008
Composer, musician, and friend
who loved this park

It was like carrying a coffin, he said.

•

In the bath, completely alone, I talk to Harris. I put him at ease, ask him with perfect calm, *Are you feeling a little crazy?*

I imagine sitting with him at the laundry on the Sunday night before his aunt brought him to the hospital for the last time. On Sunday night, the clothes tumble in the big machine. Harris sighs and—can you see the light of the small dim bulb?—hangs his head lower. I put my hand on his hand. *Do you want to go to the hospital with me now?* He isn't paranoid here, isn't violent or confused. He trusts me.

I try to spend time with our living friends, hoping it will make me miss him less.

•

Either Harris's mind or his will threw him in front of a train. I believe it was his sick mind, having temporarily overpowered his will, that coordinated his ejectment from the present into the past.

Forward onto the track, backward into the past! Think of that tidy arithmetic. It seems like a discovery, but I haven't discovered anything, once again, other than my own cleverness.

•

Harris's sister writes,

I know only a very little bit about the day Harris left the hospital. I tried to get him on the phone once I knew he'd gone in. But they had a ward phone that rings and rings and rings until one of the patients decides to answer it, and maybe if you're lucky, they'll be able to find the person you're looking for. Nobody ever answered that damned phone. And I had no number for the nurses' station. I just kept calling until I found out he'd left.

As far as I know, he'd removed his hospital bracelet and was wearing normal clothing. Even though he didn't have his cell phone or keys or anything except, it would seem, a few dollars in his pocket, he talked his way out.

I also remember that day was one of the worst rainy days of thunderstorms we had that year. Harris wandered in the rain for about ten hours before he ended up at Riverdale Station. I believe he walked there even though he had money for the train. He wasn't found with a MetroCard (that I recall). And Riverdale isn't on the subway lines.

I can only imagine what he was thinking for ten hours. If he'd set out with the intention to kill himself, he had a very long time and many possible ways to have done it. But he ran in front of a train on an outdoor platform at night in a horrible thunderstorm. Who knows what tricks his mind was playing.

This is why I believe a dybbuk killed Harris.

In Jewish folklore, dybbuks are malicious possessing spirits, the dislocated souls of the dead. They are said to have escaped from Hell, or to have been turned away from Hell for serious transgressions such as suicide, for which the soul is denied entry.

Loosely translated from the Hebrew, *dybbuk* means *attachment*. A soul unable to fulfill its function during its lifetime is given another opportunity to do so in dybbuk form. It supposedly leaves the host body once it has accomplished its goal.

Harris had spent time in Eastern Europe, traveling alone, meeting musicians. It doesn't seem impossible that he might have met a dybbuk during his travels.

The supernaturally affected musician is a familiar trope—the Italian composer and virtuoso Niccolò Paganini, for example, wrote music so difficult that in the nineteenth century it was commonly thought that he'd entered into a pact with the Devil, and in Vienna one listener declared he'd seen the Devil helping him.

Harris was a prodigy—accordion, fiddle, mandolin. Whatever he picked up he could play. It doesn't seem impossible that he might have attracted a dybbuk by his playing, and that a dybbuk who wanted to play as well as Harris might have attached to him in order to fulfill his wish. Or the dybbuk might simply have been the soul of a sinner who wished to escape the punishment of wandering the earth, and who is just trying to die, over and over.

•

I almost didn't make it. I thought this made me rare, lucky, special. How close I came! I think about the years I was sick, the weeks in intensive care, the day I almost poisoned myself—almost, almost, almost.

The memories of a few dangerous moments are smooth stones in my hand. They always feel the same.

Every time I've ever gone anywhere, I could have died. But there I was, in a car, in a plane, cheating death. Everyone alive on earth is here, cheating death at every minute. We're all the same.

Harris's father was one of the doctors who came from the suburbs to the city on the day of the attack and the days following, waiting at a hospital to treat the thousands of wounded. Hundreds of doctors waited in the wards. Everyone gave blood then, too. It felt so good to help the dead people who weren't coming.

•

I remember the smell of Harris's sour breath when we met on the subway platform of the L train at Bedford

Avenue each morning. We took the train to Union Square, then I went uptown and he went downtown, to our respective jobs.

On the subway platform of the F train at Sixth Avenue on a hot day, I remarked that the station had smelled of piss consistently since 1999. Harris smiled and said, *In fact it's smelled like that since 1998, and I know that because that's the year I started pissing here.*

For years afterward, we imitated the German store owner who'd wanted to sell him an antique mandolin: *Give it a severe thought.*

We made fun of high-concept art projects. He had a bit about an ancient bowl. *I make facsimiles of musical instruments for lost civilizations that never existed. This bowl is used to serve rice, but when it's empty, it's used to summon people to funerals . . .*

In ten years I never heard him say anything unkind about a woman.

When our frame of reference began to grow beyond what we'd learned in our expensive colleges, Harris said, smiling, not needing to explain the irony, *Eventually I stopped keeping track of how stupid I was getting.*

One year he sent Christmas cards with line drawings of Santa Claus and text beneath. *He is coming . . . The time of Moshiach is upon us!*

One of my students says, *In Scripture, people could go straight to Jesus, but with prayer, you need to be persistent.* She has laryngitis but smiles all through the week, so sure she is of her savior. She believes in a guiding force outside herself.

My life looks ridiculous next to hers. No one takes care of me. No one watches me when I sleep, but my student believes in something other than herself that doesn't want her to suffer. She believes in no excuse not to love everyone in imitation of the external thing she calls the Christ.

Under those circumstances, how does grief feel?

•

When I ask my husband for a certain notarized form for the seventh time in seven days and he says his briefcase is in another room and that he'll fetch it when he's done reading some inconsequential squib on the tiny screen of his cell phone, and when I get up and search the other room for the briefcase only to find it hung on the back of the chair he's sitting on, for just a moment I think my life wouldn't have been swallowed by disappointment if I'd married someone else—that if I'd married Harris, I would always be happy and he would have lived.

•

When my psychiatrist asked, *I know you don't take it every day, so how should I write your prescription?* I answered, *Just write "Please give Sarah all the tranquilizers she wants" and sign it.*

•

At some point I believed I might find some solace in talking to a psychic. I needed to know whether Harris was trying to talk to me and if I should prepare myself to listen.

I told my husband, who knows me all the way to the bottom of my life, or so I thought. Even now he's known me only half the time that Harris did.

When I told my husband I wanted to talk with a psychic, he accused me of having become soft and stupid, weak and sick. It gives me a headache to remember how young he seemed at that moment, and how old I felt.

Sobbing, I said, *I want to talk to Harris.* The sadder I felt, the angrier he seemed.

•

After he'd been dead a year, Harris's score to his setting of my poem "Hell" arrived in my mailbox. His friends from music school had found it while collecting his work and sent it to me, without explanation, assuming I'd been waiting for it. I hadn't known it existed, but of course I'd been waiting for it as much as I'd been waiting for any sign that Harris still wanted to talk to me, since he didn't leave a note.

•

When I asked my mother what she was thinking when she got married she said she was thinking, *Well, I'll be able to get out of this, too.* This year she and my father celebrated their sapphire anniversary.

It takes my breath away to consider that my husband may one day have known me for eleven years, not ten, and therefore longer than Harris did.

•

Suffering from nausea one day in Iowa in 1999, I took a dose of prochlorperazine, a go-to clinical antiemetic. It's an antipsychotic, too, as high-potency as haloperidol, which for decades was the gold standard. As it turns out, dopamine antagonism helps both the nauseated and the insane.

After a few minutes I felt slightly better and went to the lunch counter at the pharmacy around the corner. I'd taken prochlorperazine many times before, without any trouble, but that day, after I sat and tried to drink a Green River and eat a ninety-cent cheese sandwich, while sitting on the stool I felt an overwhelming need to move all the muscles of my body at once, continuously, in order to combat the sensation of my entire body waking up from being asleep.

I mean *asleep* in the way that a foot is said to fall asleep from pressure on a nerve pathway and on arteries that bring blood to local nerve cells. As the pressure is released and the nerve impulses readjust and the foot starts to wake up, the pins-and-needles sensation begins. Until the nerve resynchronizes with the central nervous system, the pins and needles give way to a steady burning sensation, the brain's safety strategy for a malfunctioning limb, and you have to shake your foot to put out the fire. The instinct is irresistible.

Imagine that feeling, but in your entire body.

With akathisia, you feel as if your foot has fallen asleep and has begun to wake up, but is stalled at that burning phase, that strange and painful neural overstimulation. Now imagine that instead of your foot being asleep, it's your whole body being scratched to death from the inside by a dybbuk. Others witness your torment but can't perceive the cause of it.

Clinicians write that akathisia contributes to impulsive acts of violence and suicide. According to case reports, if you have this feeling for long enough, you might jump out a window or hang yourself or stab a friend to death or murder your mother with a hammer.

·

Here are the records of three cases published in American medical journals in 1985.

Case 1: A man with chronic schizophrenia, who developed command hallucinations, received two 5 mg intramuscular injections of haloperidol over a thirty-minute period and, because of other activity in the emergency room, was left alone in a room to relax.

Within an hour he became acutely agitated and felt that he would *jump out of his skin*. He tried pacing around the room, then eloped from the emergency ward and ran home in the hope that talking with his roommates would calm the unbearable inner restlessness.

When this did not yield any relief, he went up to his third-floor apartment and leaped out of the window, breaking his leg and arm. After he was taken back to the hospital by ambulance, the symptoms of akathisia were recognized and he received an intravenous injection of diphenhydramine, which soon relieved his distress. The patient stated that he did not intend to die but would have done anything to escape the intolerable feelings induced by haloperidol. He has since steadfastly attributed his suicide attempt to the unbearable restlessness.

Case 2: The admission note by the psychiatrist stated, *He is somewhat paranoid but says he has side effects from most tranquilizers.* On the third day of hospitalization, he was referred to the psychiatrist by nurses because of difficulty getting to sleep. No evidence of aggressiveness or self-injurious behavior was charted that day in the nurses' notes. The psychiatrist prescribed haloperidol, 5 mg three times a day.

Nurses' notes that day stated, *He was very anxious about being in the hospital and threatened to kill himself if he gets up the nerve.* At 10:45 p.m., notes stated, *He has regressed during this shift in all assessment areas. His hygiene is poor.* He refused medication initially at 5:00 p.m. and stated that phenothiazines *mess me up.* He finally took the medication but then stated angrily, *Now I'll really get crazy.* He ranted loudly and profanely for thirty minutes. He took his 9:00 p.m. medication and started again, only louder and more threatening. *I'll kill all of you . . . before I leave here.*

He was found in his room at 6:50 a.m., having hanged himself with a bedsheet.

Case 3: A man received two 25 mg doses of haloperidol and was allowed to leave the hospital for an outpatient psychiatrist appointment twelve hours after admission.

One court-appointed evaluator's report described his developing symptoms of neck rigidity, arms twisting, legs being unsteady, needing to walk, and being confused. Another court-appointed psychiatrist's report stated the man had feelings that *his body was falling apart, that it was like all the bones in his body were broken, and that he was spastic and had had a minor stroke.* Repeatedly, he described his skeletal framework being out of kilter, with neck twisted and difficulty walking. *A period of loss of control, like jumping off a fence and being in mid-air* was another of his descriptions. He had been unable to sleep and stated he felt a need to get out of the approximately seventh or eighth episode of these symptoms.

It was then within thirty-six hours that he got a hammer from the basement and walked up behind his mother, striking her repeatedly, leading to her death that day.

•

When I was twenty-five my parents were exhausted from trying to prevent me from dying, which they'd already done all through my life up to that point. They'd achieved success, full marks. I was still alive.

I wanted to die and wasn't allowed to at home, so

when I was brought to the locked ward I committed myself willingly because I thought the people there would help me, though I understood the possibility of their helping me only academically. I knew that other people had gone into lockdown and come out somewhat healed, and that either outcome, healing or death, would be preferable to the way I'd been living.

Suicidal ideation is tricky. When the vision appears, it seems determined, already done. Then the vision subsides, and you see the rest of your possible life stretching out before you untainted.

If you'd asked me, on the afternoon I voluntarily committed myself, whether anything in my life outweighed the feeling that made me long for death, I would have said no, because nothing did.

It's impossible to calculate the number of good days left for a person with the kind of illness that Harris had, so maybe my belief that he would have had many more good days is a false belief.

•

Mental patients can be wily. While I was on the ward, two people managed to escape in eleven days, both having spied and memorized the lock's combination. People forget that some of the patients want to get out.

There are always at least a couple of people at the

front desk, and maybe someone who knows jujitsu, just in case. I don't know for sure.

When medication is administered, the pills are signed out and logged, then given to the patient and logged again, and while the patient takes the medicine, someone watches the pills go into the patient's mouth, and then the patient is given water to swallow, and then the patient gapes to show the pills have been swallowed. A finger is swiped under the tongue if the patient has recently been noncompliant, the clinical term for possessing a tendency to spit out pills.

Think about the person who opened the door for my dead friend. Imagine her closing it behind him.

I know it was probably a group of people at the ward's front desk, not one single person on duty when Harris left, but it feels very good to focus my attention on some imaginary wicked, murdering angel.

•

Dear angel, I feel as if I've been robbed, but there was no robbery. Harris didn't belong to me. He didn't belong to anyone.

I'd like to describe this feeling to you, angel, but no matter how close I get to it, the words that come are *disappointed* (from the French *desapointer, to derange*), *sad* (from the Middle English *saed, sated*, from the Latin *satis, enough*)—words derived from older words describing conditions of confusion or satiation, and I am neither satiated nor confused. The problem isn't just that my friend died but that I can't describe the problem according to first principles. All the words I know have lost their precision to history.

When I say *my friend had a bad death* you already know the sanctioned feelings. The knowledge arrives in a package deal, like a casket with gold-plated handles and matching gold tassels on the coverlet, which no observant Jew would ever buy. I imagine there are attempts to sell them to Jews anyway.

I want to set aside every expectation of how I should feel or act given that my friend had a bad death, and try to explain what has actually happened to me—if, in fact, anything has actually happened to me.

•

The problem with dying in private is that the rest of us don't get to watch it happen, and things that happen without us seem less real, not quite finished, maybe even impossible.

If Harris had died slowly, under a beautiful lace-trimmed coverlet, with stage four something or other, and if a yellow light had been burning somewhere in a far corner of the room as we quietly cried, and if everyone had had a chance to say goodbye or otherwise get to narrate the end of the story, then maybe I could believe that Harris is better off dead and freed from his torments.

After your friend throws himself in front of a train, you tell the rest of your friends that you love them in case they all throw themselves in front of trains before you have a chance to say it. Maybe you've said it to them before, but you do it again, just in case, as if giving them permission to forgo the lace coverlet and to die as Harris actually died—as if to say that with the lace coverlet, it would be easier.

•

My mind occasionally places me in warm midday, seated across a table from Harris, who is well and calm and maybe a little tanned, as if he has been traveling.

Since we're old friends who have been apart so long, it's always nice to run into each other. My dream is a strange town, and we're both traveling alone.

What a wonderful coincidence! *How have you been?* he asks. *I'm sorry I've haunted you. I hope it hasn't been too much trouble.*

Oh, it's no trouble at all! I say, surprised and touched. *It's just so nice to see you. Really, don't worry about it . . .*

•

I often forget I'm a particle in a cosmic process that has nothing to do with human desire or justice. I forget that the world is chaos, that it is incorruptible.

A week after he died, I wrote, *Realize a new level of not caring. What's going to happen now, Harris dies? What's to be afraid of now?*

I arrived at an appointment in Manhattan to find the entire long block cordoned. In the middle of the street was a black limousine on its side, a small mangled car far ahead of it, a brown valise, a jacket, a pair of shoes, a bloody piece of something next to the shoes. People lined the sidewalk repeating the litany of what they'd seen. It was already a myth.

•

I'm not angry at Harris for being dead.

I'm not angry at Victor. Even now, when I remember his best tattoo, a pill and a pear shaking their fists and scolding a peanut, I smile and see him smile back.

I'm not angry at my favorite aunt. I love her for eloping with a Gentile and opening a bar with him and living in the city and sending me seventy-five dollars for a coat tree when I moved to that terrible little apartment where the gunshots sounded at night.

The coats that have hung on it in these nine years! It's still here in our house in Los Angeles even though we don't wear coats as we did in New York.

•

A distant friend writes to me, having heard that Harris is dead. She writes: *I just found out about Harris's passing and wanted to send my condolences. I know he was like family to you.*

I can't measure my grief and I can't show anyone what color it is. I can offer testimony that others can reject or accept on faith, but my grief is always just my grief, unobservable by anyone but me, and then imperfectly. And maybe it isn't even grief anymore; maybe it's envy of people who aren't grieving, or shame that my grief is lasting so long when I'm not even part of Harris's family.

There are good fathers and bad fathers, good sons and bad sons, good husbands and bad ones, but great friends are all alike. We choose them and keep them. We aren't bound to them by anything but love.

It doesn't sound like much when I say my friend died. He wasn't my father or my son or my husband. *Yet there is a friend that sticketh closer than a brother*, says an Old Testament proverb.

•

We never had intercourse, but whether we had intercourse is beside the point, though if asked to identify the point, I wouldn't be able to.

I had intercourse with people I didn't know, or stopped knowing, or knew slightly, or kept knowing and kept having intercourse with, or kept knowing and stopped having intercourse with. I remember almost none of that. I remember intimacies of one kind or another, some in bed, some not.

I remember less about the embrace than about the sash a man sewed to cover a surgical wound so it wouldn't terrify us as we embraced. I remember falling out of love with a man at the same rate I fell into love with his infant son. I remember that in winter, on the treadmill at the gym, if the runner on the machine beside me and I decided wordlessly to match our pace for a mile or two, I felt a certain intimacy.

•

When a world-renowned research doctor is profiled on television, he's always shown in his lab, dripping liquid from pipettes into test tubes in a large rack. Twenty edited minutes later, he's shown sitting on a rock by the ocean, or in a field, writing poetry in a notebook, for the world-renowned research doctor is also always a poet.

I've come to call myself a doctor—not a professional doctor, of course—an amateur one. A doctor could type a novel in his spare time as easily as I could trepan a skull in my spare time. The difference is that bad surgery is a felony, whereas bad writing is merely a moral offense.

To claim oneself a writer when one is not a writer is an insult to writers, but to call oneself crazy when one is not crazy is an insult to crazy people. It belittles what they've accomplished.

•

What is grief for?

Mechanical explanation: *Pain directs my attention to an injury or insult and subsides once the injury or insult is mended or neutralized.* The pain of loss subsides if I replace what I lost or adjust permanently to accommodate the loss.

Evolutionary explanation: *Grief is a byproduct of attachment in social animals.* The grief of loss teaches me to prevent potential loss of kin.

Religious explanation: *God, the engineer of all that happens, knows best.* All life is but a gauntlet ere I live again in heaven.

Real explanation: *Love abides.* There is no other solace.

•

After a beautiful day at the beach with people who never knew Harris, all the way home, I think of opening the front door and going inside and sitting down and typing the words *Beautiful day at the beach*, and then of recording the events of the day.

But a card has come in the mail from Harris's parents that reads, *Dearest Sarah . . . There are so many things that we will never understand about Harris's life. We do know for sure that you were one of the most important people in it . . .*

•

In the Vatican Secret Archives, a woman I know examines the effects of light and heat and moisture and time on the bindings of early Italian legal and accounting documents. She is an expert on the structure, fabrication, authentication, and anti-tampering devices of these documents.

To perform her research she had to apply for admittance to Vatican City, which is guarded by boys in bright harlequin, orange and yellow and blue. They wear swords and hold staves. They stand all day at their gates, letting almost no one in.

She makes facsimiles of the documents before they decay further. She makes reality safer, but writing is never truly safe. Writing is done in a moment—the moment at which its reality is least mutable—and afterward its reality fades, approaches zero.

Nothing I perceive is real. Nothing I remember is real. I used to be able to ignore the bright light, the big fire, of that general problem. Some parts of the story are gone, but they have left a heavy imprint, and even now I can detect the shape of what made it, the shape of what used to exist.

●

Just before I fall asleep I often find myself at an imaginary party taking place in a large house. I find the shape of my grief, leaning against a doorjamb, talking to someone I know. I shudder to recognize it. I cross a threshold or climb some stairs or step down onto a porch. My mind knows not to look directly at my grief. There are many guests at the party, and it is easy to hide.

●

The first dreams were monstrous dreams, gargantuan narratives of containment and escape, lush landscapes, weird foreign countries. In one scene I saw Harris sitting in front of me, his bare back to me. I knew I mustn't startle away his ghost. I reached out, not looking, took a hand. It was his hand. I held it, our fingers interlaced. I knew he was dead. I knew it was a dream. I knew I would awaken happy.

In the last dream Harris was in a hospital, receiving medicine intravenously. He was neither dead nor alive. I begged to enter his room and I was allowed. His body wasn't human. I took his left hand, but there was no hand, just a long chicken bone stripped of meat. I spoke to him, *Aitchie . . .* The thing that was his body stirred and seemed to understand. Very softly, as I let the bone slip through my fingers, I told him goodbye. I was completely present in the dream. I knew in the dream that I could let him go, that it was the end.

•

I remember the shock of my friend Victor's death, seven years ago, as a physiological event. I doubled over and called out my denial, *no no no no no*, like an animal making its one sound.

Years later one of Victor's friends said to me, *I never got over it. After he died, I got a rash all over my body. I still have it.*

Harris has been dead three years now, but I'm quite well. I can hike in the hills, work in the garden, give a lecture, cook a meal.

Harris's mother writes, *We were told that the woman who let him out became so distraught after his death that she was unable to work again for several months.* I wish I could focus my energy on hating this distraught woman, but no feeling comes.

I still have something, though, that came with the death and never went away: *anticipatory grief*, the mourning that takes place before a certain death or loss. *A certain death or loss* refers to a terminal diagnosis, but of course you know every death is certain. We are matter. We live in matter. Within even the most metaphysical belief system we're connected to our bodies, which are matter, and which always die.

After Harris died, I decided to spend some time anticipating all the deaths I couldn't predict. I pictured my parents dead, my husband, my best friends, my relatives, everyone I knew, one by one. I started grieving good and early, so that when the deaths happened, I'd have a head start.

I work on each death. I enjoy my methodical practice. By the time the real deaths happen, I'll already have lived through them. Their assault won't shake me. Next time, I won't even need tranquilizers. Next time, I'll be ready. I'll be ready for every other death.

If I know you, you've died in my imagination. This can't be right.

•

I keep rereading my journal from the days and weeks after Harris died as if I'll find something that wasn't there the last time I read it.

On the day Harris died, I gave up the lease on the apartment I'd moved into four years earlier. Four years earlier, I'd had to travel there from another state, and

Mulder explored his new home like a burglar on the prowl. The doors rattled, the floors creaked, the window frames were rotten. A plethora of locks and grilles, all rather flimsy-looking. The bars over the bathroom window had been cut and extra padlocks added. On the kitchen table lay a big bunch of keys. But what was there to steal? No radio, no television. Just a stove weighing a ton, a rusty freezer, a washing machine, and some rickety bits of furniture. Nothing portable worth taking. Unless you counted his red suitcase. A white man's suitcase. And his laptop. The estate agent had left a note with instructions for the new occupant: *"you are safer here without luxury goods"*. Well, well. The envelope was addressed in large capitals to MR MARTEN. The name of the man he had once been. There was no getting away from it. Donald still called him by that name – Donald, the old friend who had invited him to come and see the new South Africa for himself. He also had Donald to thank for this clapped-out holiday home. The Marten of the old days was not fussy, not a man to complain of a sagging mattress or some desiccated larvae under the bedspread, nor of flecks of blood on the wall, leave aside the long flight to South Africa – squeezed in tight for a whole day – or the stomach-churning drive through the mountains. Marten took discomfort in his stride, but then he had never had to worry about tingling feet or clogged arteries. Marten didn't

Harris was there in the morning to let the movers in before I arrived.

I could write a tidy little symbolic study of this co-incidence, but now I believe that if I look hard enough at any two things, a relation will emerge. Yet an apartment doesn't replace another, and this moment doesn't replace the previous moment. It overwrites it. The tablet is illegible now, so many words written over so many other words.

•

A year after Harris died I received a letter:

> My cousin drove out to Amboy California along Route 66 and pulled his car onto the tracks moments before a freight train broadsided and killed him.
>
> He was a talented artist and appreciated your work. He had planned and rehearsed his death including his funeral where I am to read your poem "The Rider" and to comment on it.
>
> Could you please send me a copy of your poem or direct me to where I can purchase it in Canada.
> Regards,
> V. L.
> Edmonton Canada.

The first people who heard any part of this book read aloud were a group of students in a Connecticut church. One of them said to me afterward, *The date wasn't lost on me.* The next day I realized I'd read from the section about *the mundanities of July 23, 2008*, on July 23, 2010, which I would have called a coincidence if I hadn't already borne witness to enough so-called coincidences that I'd stopped trusting my understanding of the word.

I began to expect them, so when I returned to Brooklyn and visited Harris's bench in Prospect Park, I sat and waited. An orthodox Jew walked by, *payes* bobbing, the tassels of his shawl blowing around his waist, but I wasn't sure that counted. I waited until I saw a man wearing a T-shirt printed with the image of a Mondrian painting like the one Harris copied, and then I walked out of the park. As soon as I reached the sidewalk, it started raining as hard as it did on the day Harris died.

·

What if Harris died not because someone opened a door for him, but because he appeared at the threshold in the form of a doctor? Or a housefly? What if he glowed with a golden light and walked right through the door? What if he'd become invisible?

What do I wish—that I could have stopped Harris

from ending his life? That I could have given him permission to end his life, permission he didn't need? What do I regret—that in the end he didn't need me, and now I can't need him? When did I stop separating the pathological self-murdering part of him from the rest of him—at what point did I reassign the so-called self-murder to his actual self?

Why is it easier for me to think *Harris killed himself* than to think *Some unknown invasive pathology entered Harris without my knowledge and, while I wasn't looking, murdered him*?

•

I don't want to admit that I couldn't have saved Harris from his death, that I'm not magic, that I'm not special, that I won't be able to save anyone. The avocados ripen on the tree and the sun dries out the garden.

The project of life is the execution of plans during an open-ended but finite period of time. Most of us don't know how long it will be, so we don't know how to use our time most efficiently.

When I look at the veil that covers the end of my life, I feel overwhelmed by the certainty that I won't use all the time as completely as I could if I knew the date of my death. I want to give up.

From that perspective, suicide is a rational plan.

After I moved to Los Angeles, I drove a car for the first time in seven years and developed a stammer. When I took the wrong exit off a freeway and trusted my untrustworthy sense of direction and got fabulously lost and called my husband for help, I could hardly speak. As I drove home from the airport, stammering into the phone, I felt the adrenaline surging into my blood.

After I'd lived in Los Angeles for a month, someone told me that plenty of people don't use the freeways. I didn't know. I'd thought it was required. She said, *If I had to drive every day, I'd kill myself.*

I'd been making progress with my freeway panic, but as soon as she said that, I happily believed her. I no longer needed to fear I can't do what I must do, what everyone can do, that I'm a damaged, ruined person. I stopped fearing the freeway. The stammer is gone.

What if someone told me I didn't have to think about Harris anymore? *You don't have to remember him. No one else does. You never have to think about him again.*

•

The last time I saw him might have been the night that a percussionist performed a piece Harris had composed for an imaginary instrument—that is, an instrument he'd imagined and then built. It was something like a theremin.

I'd arrived late, alone, because I hadn't wanted to sit through the entire performance. I knew it would sound meaningless to my ear. I hadn't gone beyond calculus, and Harris lived in a place where math was erotic.

For a few minutes I stood outside, proud of Harris but not quite knowing whether he wanted to go to bed with the pretty percussionist, or whether he'd already gone to bed with her, or whether we should all go out together or separately. I remember thinking I should go home, that my duty to my friend was done, and in the next moment, I was introduced to a man from out of town.

The Brooklyn Inn has beautiful oriel windows and pressed metal cornices. Drinking alone one night, years ago, I saw a well-dressed man step in, order a shot, down it, place some bills on the bar, and leave without sitting down. You know it's a good bar when it attracts alcoholics with that level of familiarity.

The man from out of town and I took the train to the Brooklyn Inn, and we sat and drank and talked. As soon as I finished my drink, I put my arm around him and said *Come here*, and as soon as that happened, I knew the future, and it felt like relief. We got into a cab and went to my apartment.

We stayed awake, then slept a little, then reawoke. I called him a car and he went to the airport and back home.

•

No, I did see Harris again. He came to the Christmas party at my next apartment, the last place I lived in New York before moving to California, and he was the last guest to leave, but that isn't the last time I saw him, either, because my journal's last mention of Harris is the following March, the night I brought him to a concert uptown.

At the reception after the performance, the platter of cold cuts had no knife, so we all picked up flaps of pink meat with our hands. I remember carrying a rolled-up slice of something to the twenty-third-story balcony and looking down and then assisting a man with a bout of vertigo, but I don't remember Harris being at the reception, and I don't remember saying good night to him, or goodbye, but it was the last recorded time I ever saw him.

•

Many psychiatric patients assume that psychoactive drugs will be unpleasant. The official list of side effects—which impair memory, cognition, digestion, breathing, all the basic processes of the organism—sounds terrifying even to me, although I've taken antipsychotics every day for more than a decade and don't plan to stop.

Some time after Harris began taking his first antipsychotic, he told me he'd been feeling an unpleasant sensation for a solid week. I recognized it as akathisia.

He'd expected the pills to be poisonous, so he didn't question the side effects, didn't ask the doctor for something else, another pill, another dose, another combination. Given the known suffering of a daily pill versus the erratic but less frequent suffering of his disease, any reasonable person would choose the latter, as he did.

His sister told me he said to her, during the next-to-last year of his life, the year he tried to visit all of his faraway friends, *I don't think I'm going to live very long.*

•

I was told that Harris was nauseated and dehydrated when he was committed for the last time. He might have been given prochlorperazine, the antiemetic that gave me akathisia when I took it.

Now I think I know something of what he was thinking and feeling in those ten hours he was alone at the end of his life.

Delusional and frightened, he might reasonably have accused the doctors of drugging him with an antipsychotic, not the antiemetic they claimed it was and that carried with it the same possible torment. He might reasonably have thought that as long as he stayed in lockdown, nothing would ever stop that sensation of wild, writhing movement.

He might have left the hospital in order to be safe from the lying, malevolent doctors. He might have decided to walk off the akathisia, to wait outside the hospital in relative safety until the poisonous torment faded, but walking for ten hours might not have helped enough.

Since he was far from anyone who could give him any medicine that would counteract the akathisia, the torment and the terrible fear and the psychosis and the dehydration and the cold rain might all have readied him to listen, finally, to the voice in his head that told him, *Jump.*

•

If I'd figured this out two years ago, and if I'd found a way to communicate with Harris after he was committed, and if he were in fact given a medicine that induced akathisia, and if I'd reminded him that it was just a side effect of the wrong medicine, he might not have died.

I think I might know, now, exactly what I'm guilty of.

•

It's tempting to try to claim I've learned something very important from the experience of Harris's death, that its instruction will serve me as I continue living, that everything happens for a reason decided upon by an omniscient, omnipotent, beneficent reasoning force, which Jews are not asked to believe in, which I don't believe in, and which cannot possibly exist in the physical universe.

What I've learned from Harris's death is that I'm capable of outliving him—and that I might live a long time, now that he's so violently reduced the statistical likelihood of my own self-dispatch.

•

One more day at the beach, just the five of us from Chambers Street. Harris drives us in his parents' car. Loud music plays. He sings to every song. He turns up the volume. Heat mirrors the road.

At the beach the sand reflects the sun. We burn ourselves on both sides and swim in the ocean. One of the others tells me to stop smiling so hard, to try to contain myself, but I can't. *It looks insincere*, he says. I'm smiling now, remembering. Still smiling.

Harris is just a shimmer, a null set. He reflects my grief, and it's so bright I can't see much behind it, but behind the brightness is a human shape.

I look at him, then look away. I was so lucky.

3   *The Thursday edition of the* Riverdale Press: See Megan James, "Man Struck by Train Is Identified."

12   *"I'm not sure that anyone"*: Emily L. Senecal, e-mail exchange with the author, 2010.

32   *The dictionary defines psychosis*: See *Merriam-Webster's Collegiate Dictionary*

32   *The clinical definition narrows*: Ibid.

33   *The dimensional approach to defining psychosis*: See H. J. Eysenck, "Classification and the Problems of Diagnosis."

34   torment, restlessness, pulling or drawing: See R. E. Drake and J. Ehrlich, "Suicide Attempts Associated with Akathisia." "Some of the best definitions of akathisia come from the medical literature on the use of reserpine as an antihypertensive in the mid-1950s." See David Healy, Andrew Herxheimer, and David B. Menkes, "Antidepressants and Violence: Problems at the Interface of Medicine and Law." "Akathisia has two components: subjective (psychological) and objective (motor)." See E. Szabadi, "Akathisia—or Not Sitting."

35   *"the patient could not remain sitting down"*: From Ladislav Haškovec, "L'akathisie."

36   *one of the chamberlains of Napoleon III*: From G. E. Berrios, "Lad Haškovec and Akathisia: An Introduction."

36   *Akathisia became clinically relevant in the 1950s*: See Martin Brüne, "Ladislav Haškovec and 100 years of Akathisia."

36   *The condition seemed to result more frequently at higher doses*: "Neurology textbooks of the pre-antipsychotic era described akathisia in Parkinsonian patients, and the importance of the term has further increased after the introduction of antipsychotics in the 1950s." From Pavel

Mohr and Jan Volavka, "Ladislav Haškovec and Akathisia: 100th Anniversary."

36 *Some studies now show upwards of 75 percent*: "Akathisia is common in general medical settings, especially when patients are taking antiemetics. In cancer patients undergoing chemotherapy, 50 percent of patients met the diagnostic threshold of akathisia, yet 75 percent stated they would not have reported the symptoms of akathisia." See Hiroko Akagi and T. Manoj Kumar, "Akathisia: Overlooked at a Cost."

36 Extraordinary suffering: Akathisia has been well documented as a common and distressing side effect of antipsychotic drugs and an important cause of poor drug compliance. See Akagi and Kumar, "Akathisia." See Thomas R. E. Barnes, "A Rating Scale for Drug-Induced Akathisia." See Healy, Herxheimer, and Menkes, "Antidepressants and Violence." "Failure to identify and treat this disorder can result in extraordinary suffering for the patient, which can in turn lead to preoccupation with the idea of suicide, specifically by jumping." See M. Sabaawi, T. F. Holmes, and M. R. Fragala, "Drug-Induced Akathisia: Subjective Experience and Objective Findings."

37 *when symptoms develop gradually*: From Emily L. Senecal.

37 *without adequate clinical supervision*: "Used ineptly or without adequate clinical supervision, [antipsychotic drugs] can cause akathisia, an extremely uncomfortable state of agitation, muscle discomfort, and a difficulty in sitting still (often described by patients as feeling as if they are 'jumping out of their skin')." See Kay Redfield Jamison, *Night Falls Fast*.

37 *mania*: See Barnes, "A Rating Scale for Drug-Induced Akathisia."

37 *anger*: See Drake and Ehrlich, "Suicide Attempts Associated with Akathisia."

37 *overwhelmingly identified as homicide and suicide*: See Drake and Ehrlich, "Suicide Attempts Associated with Akathisia." See Healy, Herxheimer, and Menkes, "Antidepressants and Violence." See J. R. Schulte, "Homicide and Suicide Associated with Akathisia and Haloperidol."

37 *specifically by jumping*: "Failure to identify and treat this disorder can result in extraordinary suffering for the patient, which can in turn lead to preoccupation with the idea of suicide, specifically by jumping." See Sabaawi, Holmes, and Fragala, "Drug-Induced Akathisia."

38   I can hear the music all around me: Dudley Moore, last words as reported by Rena Fruchter in her book *Dudley Moore: An Intimate Portrait*.

43   *When a male child is born*: See Esther Hecht, Official site of the Maltese Jewish Community.

58   *One of us would ask*: Woody Allen, *Annie Hall*.

58   *Statistics show that suicides*: Centers for Disease Control and Prevention, National Vital Statistics System, Mortality Tables.

59   *In one of them, she wrote*: From "Three Songs" (part III): See Rachel Wetzsteon, lines from "Three Songs."

80   *Clinicians write that akathisia*: See Healy, Herxheimer, and Menkes, "Antidepressants and Violence"; Sabaawi, Holmes, and Fragala, "Drug-Induced Akathisia"; and Schulte, "Homicide and Suicide."

81   *Case 1: A man with chronic schizophrenia*: See Drake and Ehrlich, "Suicide Attempts Associated with Akathisia."

82   *Case 2: The admission note*: See Schulte, "Homicide and Suicide."

83   *Case 3: A man received two 25 mg doses*: See Schulte, "Homicide and Suicide."

BIBLIOGRAPHY

Akagi, Hiroko, and T. Manoj Kumar. "Akathisia: Overlooked at a Cost." *British Medical Journal* 324:7352 (22 June 2002): 1506–07.

Allen, Woody. *Annie Hall.* Film, 93 minutes. MGM/UA, 1977.

Barnes, Thomas R. E. "A Rating Scale for Drug-Induced Akathisia." *British Journal of Psychiatry* 154 (1989): 672–76.

Berrios, G. E. "Lad Haškovec and Akathisia: An Introduction." *History of Psychiatry* 6 (June 1995): 243–51.

Brüne, Martin. "Ladislav Haškovec and 100 Years of Akathisia." *American Journal of Psychiatry* 159:5 (May 2002): 727.

Centers for Disease Control and Prevention. National Vital Statistics System, Mortality Tables. www.cdc.gov/nchs/nvss/mortality_tables .htm.

Drake, R. E., and J. Ehrlich. "Suicide Attempts Associated with Akathisia." *American Journal of Psychiatry* 142 (1985): 599–601.

Eysenck, H. J. "Classification and the Problems of Diagnosis." In *Handbook of Abnormal Psychology*, edited by H. J. Eysenck, 1–31. London: Pitman, 1960.

Fruchter, Rena. *Dudley Moore: An Intimate Portrait.* London: Ebury Press, 2004.

Giuliani, Rudolph. Press conference speech (11 September 2001).

Godard, Jean-Luc. *A bout de souffle.* Film, 90 minutes. Les Productions Georges de Beauregard, 1960.

Haškovec, Ladislav. "L'akathisie." *Revue Neurologique* 9 (1901): 1107–09. Translated from the French by G. E. Berrios.

———. "Nouvelles remarques sur l'akathisie." *Nouvelle Iconographie de la Salpêtrière* 14 (1903): 287–96.

Healy, David, Andrew Herxheimer, and David B. Menkes. "Antidepressants and Violence: Problems at the Interface of Medicine and Law." *PLoS Medicine* 3:9 (September 2006): 1478–87.

Hecht, Esther. Official site of the Maltese Jewish Community. www.jewsof malta.org.

James, Megan. "Man Struck by Train Is Identified." *Riverdale Press* (7 August 2008).

Jamison, Kay Redfield. *Night Falls Fast*, p. 250. New York: Random House, 1999.

Journal of the American Medical Association 43 (27 August 1904): 622.

Merriam-Webster's Collegiate Dictionary, Eleventh Edition. Definitions of *psych-* and *-osis*.

———. Definition of *psychosis*.

Mohr, Pavel, and Jan Volavka. "Ladislav Haškovec and Akathisia: 100th Anniversary." *British Journal of Psychiatry* 181 (2002): 537.

Sabaawi, M., T. F. Holmes, and M. R. Fragala. "Drug-Induced Akathisia: Subjective Experience and Objective Findings." *Military Medicine* 159:4 (April 1994): 286–91.

Schulte, J. R. "Homicide and Suicide Associated with Akathisia and Halo-peridol." *American Journal of Forensic Psychiatry* 6 (1985): 3–7.

Senecal, Emily L. E-mail exchange with the author, 2010.

Szabadi, E. "Akathisia—or Not Sitting." *British Medical Journal* 202 (19 April 1986): 1034–35.

Wetzsteon, Rachel. Lines from "Three Songs." *The Other Stars*. New York: Penguin, 1994.

ACKNOWLEDGMENTS

The author acknowledges the American Academy of Arts and Letters, the American Academy in Rome, Adam Chapman, Maggie Nelson, Domenick Ammirati, Mitzi Angel, Chantal Clarke, Kathy Daneman, Jeremy Dauber, Matt Haber, Ben Herzog, Sheila Heti, Chelsea Hodson, Mishka Jaeger, Jennifer L. Knox, Nick Laird, Alan Lyman, Judith and Frank Manguso, PJ Mark, Jenny Moore, Ed Park, Emily Senecal, Michal Shavit, David Shields, David M. Sollors, Lorin Stein, Deb Olin Unferth, Carol and Howard Wulfson, and the editors of the *Seattle Review*, where a portion of this book was published in a slightly different form under the title "Class Note."

111